The Professional Teacher

Agenda for Education in a Democracy
Timothy J. McMannon, Series Editor

The Professional Teacher

The Preparation and Nurturance of the Reflective Practitioner

Kay A. Norlander-Case
Timothy G. Reagan
Charles W. Case

Agenda for Education in a Democracy

Volume 4

Jossey-Bass Publishers
San Francisco

Jossey-Bass books and products are available through most bookstores. To contact Jossey-Bass directly, call (888) 378–2537, fax to (800) 605–2665, or visit our website at www.josseybass.com.

Substantial discounts on bulk quantities of Jossey-Bass books are available to corporations, professional associations, and other organizations. For details and discount information, contact the special sales department at Jossey-Bass.

 Manufactured in the United States of America on Lyons Falls Turin Book. This paper is acid-free and 100 percent totally chlorine-free.

Library of Congress Cataloging-in-Publication Data

Norlander-Case, Kay A., 1949–
  The professional teacher : the preparation and nurturance of the reflective practitioner / Kay A. Norlander-Case, Timothy G. Reagan, Charles W. Case.
    p. cm.—(Agenda for education in a democracy; v. 4)
  Includes bibliographical references and index.
  ISBN 0-7879-4560-9 (pbk.)
  1. Teachers—Training of—United States. 2. Teachers—In-service training—United States. 3. Action research in education—United States. I. Reagan, Timothy G. II. Case, Charles W. III. Title. IV. Series.
  LB1715.N54   1999
  370'.71'1—dc21

                                                            99-6257

PB Printing   10 9 8 7 6 5 4 3 2 1   FIRST EDITION

Contents

Series Foreword

In 1894, a young Theodore Roosevelt proclaimed, "There are two gospels which should be preached to every reformer. The first is the gospel of morality; the second is the gospel of efficiency."[1] The interplay of efficiency and morality in human institutions, particularly in the educational institutions we call schools, continues to intrigue.[2] On the surface, both morality and efficiency are good; *morality* denotes fairness, virtue, and good conduct, among other things, and *efficiency* bespeaks a high level of achievement or production with a minimal expenditure of effort, money, or time. Ideally, our schools, our governments, our places of employment, even our families would be both moral and efficient in their own ways.

Difficulties arise, however, when we attempt to move beyond generalizations to specifics. What is morality? Who decides? Philosophers far wiser than I have spent lifetimes trying to convince themselves and others that there are or there are not definitive answers to those brief but complex questions. How can efficiency be judged? What are the criteria? Again the questions point to no single, certain answers. Moreover, inefficiencies have frequently been imposed on human institutions in the name of efficiency, and immoralities promulgated in the name of morality. When we advance to another level of specificity and consider morality and efficiency in the schools, the questions not only retain their complexity but also become very personal and deadly serious: Should my child's school teach morality? What exactly would that mean? How efficient is the schooling my child is experiencing? Do my child's grades reflect actual learning? These and similar questions shape debates and decisions about our nation's schools.

Neil Postman argues that we come to understand our lives and ascribe meaning to our actions by placing them in the context of a narrative: "a story . . . that tells of origins and envisions a future, a story that constructs ideals, prescribes rules of conduct, provides a source of authority, and, above all, gives a sense of continuity and purpose."[3] If Postman is right—and I think he is—then our chosen narratives help both to determine and to reveal what we are willing to work for, to live for, perhaps even to die for.

Rarely, if ever, are people called on to give their lives in defense of the institution of the school or the process of education. Some heroic teachers have, of course, given their lives in defense of their students. Clearly their narratives embraced selflessness and sacrifice. But for most educators, selflessness and sacrifice mean no more than forgoing other more lucrative and respected professions, giving up evenings and weekends to grade papers, or serving on interminable committees. Even these sacrifices represent hardships, however, and they raise questions about educators' narratives. What are teachers willing to work for, to give their lives *to*?

Educators in the sixteen settings of the National Network for Educational Renewal (NNER)—be they school faculty, teacher educators, or arts and sciences professors—have chosen to embrace a morally based narrative for education and schooling. They see schools as places where democracy is learned and practiced, where schooling is far more than job training, where education is a seamless process of self-improvement. To them, teaching must be guided by a four-part mission: enculturating the young in a social and political democracy, providing access to knowledge for all children and youths, practicing a nurturant pedagogy, and ensuring responsible stewardship of the schools. Each part of the mission is based on and permeated by moral dimensions.[4]

Because they perceive all levels of schooling to be interconnected, NNER educators insist that the improvement of the nation's schools and the improvement of its teacher education programs must proceed simultaneously. Having better schools requires having better teachers; preparing better teachers requires having exemplary schools in which to prepare them. And the word *reform* rarely enters NNER educators' vocabularies: that term implies a finite process with corruption at one end and completion at the other. Faculty members at NNER settings prefer to think of educational improvement as a process of *renewal* by which they continuously remake good schools and teacher education programs into better ones through inquiry and hard work. NNER participants work toward the simultaneous renewal of schooling and the education of educators.

Without a plan, simultaneous renewal would be no more than a slogan. In other words, it would be morality without efficiency. The plan, or agenda, by which NNER educators pursue simultaneous renewal has come to be called the Agenda for Education in a Democracy. No creation of momentary inspiration, the Agenda emerged over several years as a product of inquiries into schools and teaching, and it was disseminated by means of several books written or edited by John Goodlad and his associates. Goodlad's *A Place Called School* (1984) began the process of explicating the Agenda, and four books published in 1990—*The Moral Dimensions of Teaching, Places Where Teachers Are Taught, Teachers for Our Nation's Schools,* and *Access to Knowledge*—further developed the essential concepts.[5] These concepts were clarified for implementation as nineteen postulates, which describe conditions that must be established in order to achieve the four-part mission for educators and the schools in which they teach.[6] The postulates guide the efforts of school and university leaders as they work together to establish new organizational structures and processes to advance their institutions on the path of simultaneous renewal.

The books in the Agenda for Education in a Democracy series explore key ideas underlying the Agenda and describe strategies for pursuing the simultaneous renewal of schools and the education of educators. In *The Professional Teacher: The Preparation and Nurturance of the Reflective Practitioner*, Kay A. Norlander-Case, Timothy G. Reagan, and Charles W. Case argue that teaching is a moral profession requiring not only extensive preservice preparation but also continuous in-service development. It is particularly important, they assert, that teachers have the opportunity and capacity to reflect seriously on their work and, as stewards of schools, to effect change in the schools and in themselves. *The Professional Teacher* draws heavily on the authors' own experiences as members of the faculty of the School of Education at the University of Connecticut and on their students' journals and other writings. The result is a powerful description of a teacher education program firmly anchored in both the university and the schools. This account reveals that morally based teacher preparation can be efficient as well.

TIMOTHY J. MCMANNON
Series Editor
Agenda for Education
in a Democracy

Foreword

One can make a strong case for the proposition that the struggle of schools, colleges, and departments of education (SCDEs) for scholarly recognition and accompanying status in higher education has deflected them from their traditional role in teacher education and has slowed the emergence of teaching as a profession. In the sample of teacher-preparing settings that my colleagues and I studied in the late 1980s, we found professors of education in most colleges and universities pulling back from the role in teacher education for which they had originally been employed in order to meet the growing pressure for research and publication. We found that middle-range universities preparing large numbers of teachers increasingly were following the pattern already established in heavily research-oriented institutions in assigning parts of their teacher education programs to adjunct, temporary faculty members. The name of the game for tenure-track faculty was publish, publish, publish—and then advance to teaching graduate courses more easily connected with their research.

One could argue that by heeding the drumbeat increasingly driving their colleagues in the arts and sciences, professors of education were producing the body of specialized knowledge that teaching must have if it is to warrant recognition as a profession. The problem, however, is that the connections between this knowledge and both the practice and the policy arenas of schooling and the education it is supposed to enlighten have been weak. Until quite recently, the dance toward scholarship in education has been away from research on both the conduct of teacher education and the renewing processes necessary to all robust professional preparation programs. Teacher preparation is not the only endeavor of professional education for which this description applies, but it is one of the most sharply etched.

The emergence of teacher education as a robust university enterprise has been hampered by what has been referred to as "status deprivation." With progression from normal school to teachers college (giving attention to teacher education as the primary institutional commitment and often with an elementary and secondary school and their teachers on campus), and then to state college and university, our tertiary educational institutions dropped teacher education lower and lower in their priorities. By the mid-1980s, the business school was becoming the crown jewel on the campuses of many universities, often attracting funds for a clutch of endowed chairs. One would have had to look very hard for endowed professorships in teacher education. The top-ranked schools of education, all in major research-oriented universities, prepared only a handful of teachers or none. Oddly, some recent selections of "outstanding" teacher education programs appear to have equated the reputation of a near-nonexistent teacher education program with the high ranking of the institution among Research I universities in the Carnegie classification system. A relatively small institution such as Maryville University in St. Louis, with a first-rate teacher education program producing far more teachers, apparently is not in the running.

Given the legacy of teacher education as a low-status enterprise pushed to the periphery of attention as universities aspire for Research I or II classification (and their schools of education gain increased scholarly recognition), the story that follows in this book of the Agenda for Education in a Democracy series emerges as remarkable. Here we have a flagship research university, the University of Connecticut, sending a message regarding the importance of teacher education by taking on a daunting agenda of comprehensively renewing its existing program. The message goes particularly to its peer institutions nationwide. It is a moral message that challenges the affront that teacher education is the responsibility of "lesser" universities that are not yet doctoral granting and not yet ranked high for their research.

The challenge to renewal in teacher education rises out of much more than the legacy of low status and neglect not yet transcended, in spite of the growing awareness of the connection between better teachers and better schools. Inattention to the curriculum of preparation has been the companion, if not the result, of inattention to the enterprise in general. The state role in teacher licensing and program approval, frequently bureaucratic in implementation, has rarely been productive of creativity in the curricular domain. In our research (reported in my *Teachers for Our Nation's Schools* in 1990), directors of teacher education in several of the institutions we visited were simply checking off newly announced state requirements against existing courses, to which they added or from which they dropped topics in the syllabi.[1] Professors told us that they had been around the track of serious curricular revision a couple of times before, only to have their hard work negated by new state regulations. They were not about to go around again. Add this context to that of the institutional signals that scholarly productivity is the primary criterion for promotion, and one begins to understand, if not appreciate, the lethargy that commonly has prevailed in the domain of curricular planning.

For decades it was easy to predict the teacher education curriculum one would find in colleges and universities: a course or two in the historical, philosophical, and social foundations of education; one in psychology; another in the general methods of teaching; and then six to ten weeks of student teaching for all future teachers, but with a chunk taken out of the arts and sciences added to the education of the future elementary school teacher for courses in the content and methods of teaching an array of school subjects. When I visited a number of teacher-preparing institutions in 1961 and

1962 as a member of the team I helped James B. Conant put together, this was the curriculum we found quite uniformly. When I
visited colleges and universities with another team in 1987 and
1988, this framework was still the mode, but much of the historical
and philosophical grounding that had characterized the foundations
courses more than a quarter of a century before had been replaced
by a grab bag of topics designed to help orient new teachers to the
expectations and requirements of teaching—from maintaining class
records to meeting licensing requirements to observing legal re-
straints. There was somewhat more attention to school visitations
and classroom observations and more time devoted to student teaching. The curricular circumstances of the early 1960s and the late
1980s were startlingly similar in their failure to immerse future teachers in serious discourse about the mission of schooling in our social
and political democracy and their role in advancing it. They were
equally lacking in the critical introspection that accompanies all
processes of educational renewal. There was evaluation of teachers-
to-be, almost exclusively in the academic domain, but little ongoing evaluation of their preparation programs.

Little research is needed to deduce considerable agreement on
the major commonsense components of the professional preparation program of future teachers and wide disagreement on the balance of their distribution. There are the general education and
subject specialization that take place in the arts and sciences departments of the university, the pedagogical component conceded
to SCDEs, and supervised practice in school classrooms. Presumably, coherent curricula bind all three into adherence to a guiding
mission. But research reveals that this presumption is ill founded.
Perhaps a mission is assumed, but it is rarely articulated or discussed.
The three groups listed do not constitute a designated responsible
faculty, and they certainly do not routinely come together in discussion of mission and program renewal.

Enough already! Colleagues and I have collated from our research and that of others a litany of need that cries out for attention, moral commitment, and human engineering. By joining

empirical inquiry with that of deduction from moral principle regarding the good life in the good society, we have fashioned a daunting agenda of renewal—the Agenda for Education in a Democracy—that combines mission, necessary conditions to be put in place, and strategy. This last requires the symbiotic synthesis of the three now-separated faculties into just one—from the arts and sciences, from the SCDEs, and from the P–12 partner schools that provide teaching experiences—in the simultaneous renewal of schooling and the education of educators (as described in the first volume of this series, *Leadership for Educational Renewal*).

Unlike so many of the appeals to educational reform—"Get on board the train, and then we'll talk about where we are going and what is required of you"—the Agenda for Education in a Democracy was spelled out in considerable detail at the time of its first presentation in the early 1990s and juxtaposed against the backdrop of the ethos and accompanying circumstances likely to make its implementation exceedingly difficult. Parts of the Agenda are sufficiently challenging to invoke familiar excuses for opting out of addressing it: "We're doing all that already" or "We tried that years ago, and it didn't work." We have in our files a few letters affirming this self-congratulatory fantasy.

We also have in our records information that led a colleague to communicate with some 250 teacher-preparing settings that expressed interest in joining the National Network for Educational Renewal (NNER) that we had created to test-drive the Agenda. Over several months, nearly 60 of these went through a demanding admissions process that required, among other things, sustained attention to and discussion of the Agenda's mission and the conditions of and for teacher education it requires (in nineteen propositions referred to as postulates).

The Agenda for Education in a Democracy and the NNER emerged out of research and development conducted by the Center for Educational Renewal (CER) at the University of Washington from the CER's founding in 1985 into the early 1990s. The translation of this Agenda into the curriculum of a leadership training program was then carried out by the independent Institute for Educational Inquiry (IEI), founded in 1992. Those of us on the staff of the CER and the IEI have had the opportunity to be closely associated with the settings of the NNER from the time of their initial commitment to the Agenda. This association has brought us into intimate involvement with the varying processes of educational renewal in the participating colleges and universities and their many collaborating school districts and partner schools. In effect, we have been colleagues, uniquely privy to firsthand experiences and conversations from which outside evaluators and researchers often are excluded. The lessons learned are many and powerful.

There is nothing surprising in the observation that comprehensive renewal of longstanding programmatic regularities in an ethos of the sort described earlier is an uphill struggle. The metaphors invoked are "going against the grain," "walking upstream," and "running into the wind." Much less obvious are the characteristics of the changing ethos necessary to progress. These are the essentials of the ecology of renewal that Seymour Sarason, Michael Fullan, Kenneth Sirotnik, and others have studied and described. The obstacles tend to be most formidable in the early stages. The resolution to continue depends heavily on a leadership core of individuals able to articulate the mission clearly and bring into play whatever supportive resources can be mustered. It was imperative for those of us in the CER and the IEI who carried moral responsibility for engaging others in the initiative to demonstrate our belief in the Agenda and our faith in the core groups of leaders in each of the NNER settings. But with progress and optimism increasingly transcending frustration and pessimism, our supportive role became less one of providing technical support while we continued to massage the concepts and principles of our common endeavor. The high in successful *renewal* comes in large part from a growing sense of personal efficacy. In *reform*, by contrast, the best the implementer can hope for is the dubious satisfaction of compliance. Ironically, it is the reformer who reaps the rewards.

The books in this series contain narratives that enrich our understanding of individual, institutional, and programmatic renewal. This book, focused on a single NNER setting, is comprehensive in its account of what goes into the substance and process of preparing the professional educator, from selection to induction into teaching. The story that unfolds in the collaboration of the University of Connecticut and several schools is one of redesigning virtually every component into something quite different from what existed before without stopping the traffic of future teachers from crossing the bridge to practice.

Two matters not readily apparent in the narrative stand out among the many addressed. One is the absence of criticism of those often described as naysayers. We know that many individuals who draw back from participation in broad-scale change and even those strong in their criticism are not villains predisposed to obstruction. Some are simply uncertain about the fate of courses into which they have put a great deal of effort and which they teach well. Some who were active in previous efforts that dissipated when the leaders defected are skittish about getting involved one more time. These often are people with much talent to bring to the initiative, once convinced that the effort is worthwhile and destined to have longevity. It is folly to turn them off by striking back harshly because of their apparent reservations.

The second matter that might escape attention pertains to a negative response that came to our attention quite early in the initiative: "I can't get involved in an effort like this because it will get in the way of my research." We have some evidence to suggest that this complaint, when voiced, came quite often from faculty members not much involved in research. The complaint sounds very much like that of the chronic naysayer. Faculty members productive of research and publication at the beginning of their institution's participation in the NNER appear to remain actively involved still. The three authors of this book, all leaders in the renewing process, have demonstrated in their own work the productive inquiry it stimulated. John Dewey reminded us years ago that the inquiry leading to a science of education begins and ends in practice.

A 1998 review of dozens of studies of teaching and teacher education concludes that there has been and commonly remains a disconnection between the preparation teachers receive and the circumstances they encounter in schools and classrooms.[2] The research my colleagues and I have conducted, on which the Agenda for Education in a Democracy is partly based, led to the same conclusion. I do not argue that teacher preparation (or any other professional education) should fit precisely with existing practice. If it did, practice would stagnate. But beginning practitioners, with their eyes on a clear mission, must be able to cope with the circumstances they encounter and move them to a higher plane. Many neophytes do not last in teaching beyond the first three years.

Two kinds of information encourage us to believe that what is happening in the school-university partnership of which the University of Connecticut is a part represents a productive coupling of preparation and practice. The many narratives of prospective teachers in the program speak to this, as do the evaluative studies increasingly being reported in theses and dissertations of graduate students. This part of the overall story is particularly unique and creative.

It also becomes apparent that, transcending the whole and constituting its spine, is the introspective inquiry described in Chapter Two and implicit throughout the rest of the book. An ethos of critical self-appraisal is as characteristic of renewal as its lack is to individual, institutional, and societal stagnation. What is most worthy of continued critical attention and retention in the Connecticut setting and each of the others in the National Network for Educational Renewal is not an exemplary program in place but an infrastructure of educational renewal in progress.

Seattle, Washington   JOHN I. GOODLAD
April 1999

Acknowledgments

Renewing schools and the programs that prepare future educators in ways that are morally grounded is a responsibility of all who call themselves teachers or teacher educators. The task is one that often perplexes us. But then there are those such as John Goodlad who have given us the hope, courage, and intellectual guidance necessary to move forward and to act in professionally moral ways. Without John, the strides that we have been able to take in advancing the agenda of simultaneous renewal of schools and the education of future teachers would have been next to impossible. It was always John and his equally dedicated colleagues at the Center for Educational Renewal, at the Institute for Educational Inquiry, and throughout the National Network for Educational Renewal who helped us "worry" about the issues that mattered most. He was the one who started us on this journey of conversation about the moral dimensions of our profession. John, we thank you more than you will ever know.

We are also most grateful to a large cadre of professional educators from the Hartford Public Schools. Teachers and administrators alike have assisted us over a ten-year period in addressing school change and the education of teachers. These individual teachers and school principals, along with the students in five schools—Batchelder School, Bulkeley High School, Dwight Elementary, Maria Sanchez Elementary, and Quirk Middle School—have demonstrated over and over again that teachers are professionals.

There are too many teachers to name here, and that is the wonder of it: that there are so many great teachers in these five schools that it would take many pages to list them all.

One person must be acknowledged for beginning the partnership between the Hartford Public Schools and the School of Education at the University of Connecticut. When we first came to work in Hartford, it was Anna Salamone Consoli who greeted us. Ten years ago she was the principal of Bulkeley High School. She welcomed us with open arms and with questions that she wished to have answered: "How can we change schooling such that it is equitable and productive for all?" and "How can we ensure that teachers, both beginning and seasoned, are supported to act in professional ways?" Since that first meeting, Anna has fostered caring environments in which such questions continue to be addressed. Anna, much of what we know about schools and preparing educators comes from you. Your voice is always with us.

And now we move on to the next generation of professional educators. We thank our students at the University of Connecticut who have contributed their words and actions in making this book come alive. But it is more than your contribution to the book that we wish to thank you for. We acknowledge your persistent dedication and courage; your work has changed and will continue to change the educational experience for so many children and youths in your care. You have lent your stories so graciously. Each of you is the type of professional educator whom John Goodlad would be proud of—and we are proud of you too.

Finally, when it came time to put it all together, it was Tim McMannon, the series editor, who lent his expertise, as did Paula McMannon and Amanda Froh, who were always ready and willing to respond to our many calls for assistance.

April 1999   KAY A. NORLANDER-CASE
                                                    TIMOTHY G. REAGAN
                                                    CHARLES W. CASE

About the Sponsor

The National Network for Educational Renewal (NNER) was established in 1986 to put into practice the belief that the improvement of schooling and the renewal of teacher education must proceed simultaneously. In short, good schools require good teachers, and good teachers learn their profession in good schools.

The NNER presently embraces sixteen member settings in fourteen states: California, Colorado, Connecticut, Hawaii, Maine, Missouri, Nebraska, New Jersey, Ohio, South Carolina, Texas, Utah, Washington, and Wyoming. Member settings work to build collaboration among three main groups that play a vital role in the preparation of new teachers: education faculty in colleges and universities; arts and sciences faculty; and faculty in elementary and secondary schools. All told, there are thirty-three colleges or universities, over one hundred school districts, and about five hundred partner schools in the NNER.

The NNER extends the work of the Center for Educational Renewal (CER), which was founded in 1985 by John I. Goodlad, Kenneth A. Sirotnik, and Roger Soder to study and facilitate "the simultaneous renewal of schooling and the education of educators."

To support the work of the NNER and the CER, Goodlad, Soder, and Sirotnik established the independent, nonprofit Institute for Educational Inquiry (IEI) in Seattle in 1992. The IEI oversees leadership training programs for key personnel from NNER settings, administers grants from philanthropic organizations to the NNER, conducts research and evaluation studies, and publishes a series of Work in Progress papers. The IEI is the sponsoring agency for the Agenda for Education in a Democracy series.

About the Authors

The Authors

Kay A. Norlander-Case is an associate professor of special education in the Department of Educational Psychology, School of Education, University of Connecticut. Since 1971 she has taught special education, coordinated a program for college students with learning disabilities, administered federal grants in the areas of teacher education and learning disabilities, and participated in improving teacher education. She has spent the past nine years working in partnership schools in Hartford, Connecticut. She has published book chapters and articles in the areas of teacher education, urban education, and special education and has presented over ninety papers on these topics at national and regional meetings. She was a member of Cohort II of the Institute for Educational Inquiry's Leadership Associates Program (1992–1993). Her areas of research interest include school-university partnerships, urban education, the inclusion of students with special education needs, and teacher education.

Timothy G. Reagan is professor in the Language, Literacy and Society Program in the Department of Curriculum and Instruction at the University of Connecticut. He has taught and published in a number of areas, including applied linguistics, comparative and international education, multicultural education, and foreign language education. Much of his work has focused on the education of cultural and linguistic minority groups in the United States and elsewhere. He is well known for his analyses of the deaf as a cultural and linguistic minority group, as well as for his work on language policy in the educational sphere. He is the author of *Non-Western Educational Traditions* (1996) and coauthor of *Becoming a Reflective Educator: How to Build a Culture of Inquiry in the Schools* (1994). He was a member of Cohort II of the Institute for Educational Inquiry's Leadership Associates Program (1992–1993).

Charles W. Case is professor in the School of Education at the University of Connecticut. Since 1960 he has been a secondary school English teacher, an administrator in a regional educational service center, an administrator and teacher in community colleges, a department chair, and a dean and professor in four universities. He has been involved in school-university partnerships since 1967. He has written over one hundred books, chapters, articles, and monographs on teacher education, school-university partnerships, planning and urban education, organizational and community development, desegregation, and educational policy.

The Contributors

John I. Goodlad is president of the Institute for Educational Inquiry and codirector of the Center for Educational Renewal at the University of Washington. Throughout his career, he has been involved in an array of educational renewal programs and projects and has engaged in large-scale studies of educational change, schooling, and teacher education. In addition to advancing a comprehensive program of research and development directed to the simultaneous renewal of schooling and teacher education, he is inquiring into the mission of education in a democratic society.

Timothy J. McMannon is a senior associate of the Institute for Educational Inquiry and of the Center for Educational Renewal at the University of Washington and teaches history at colleges and universities in the Seattle area. His main areas of interest include recent U.S. history, the history of American education, and the public purpose of education and schooling.

*We dedicate this book to those educators
who stand apart through their actions and intellect,
particularly Cathleen Case Rosenzweig, Jo Ann Freiberg,
Sue Rosenfield, and Michael Rosenzweig.*

Introduction:
Earning the Right to Teach

For teaching to be recognized and respected as a profession, we must first recognize, as Kathleen Devaney and Gary Sykes suggest, that it must earn that right: "Developing a work culture that is professional must be done in partnership with the workers themselves—teachers. Professionalism is a form of liberty that is not simply conferred; it is earned. Teachers themselves must not only be enabled; they must be convinced that tasks in their work can be accomplished only under professional standards, norms, and conditions. Then teachers themselves must set about achieving these."[1]

A profession cannot exist without a serious and committed group of individuals who constitute its membership. To earn the "liberty" of being called professionals, educators must not only adhere to standards; they must uphold and advance the moral dimensions inherent in serving others. Members of a true teaching profession must have knowledge and technical competence; share values about their profession and its consequent responsibilities; carry out inquiry and reflection as a matter of course; recognize, celebrate, and take into account diversity in the provision of equitable educational opportunities to all children; and have an altruism toward their profession that will enable it to grow and prosper. They must be open-minded thinkers who have chosen to become educators and strongly believe that they will not advantage children to become citizens in a democracy without first educating teachers in a tradition of inquiry and understanding of others. This very different tradition of teaching relies on teachers who are liberally educated, have a propensity for questioning and reflection, have a capacity to nurture those in their care, understand democratic values and responsibilities, and, above all, are committed to a set of moral principles on which the teaching profession can ground itself. Such caring, nurturing, and knowledgeable teachers would collectively have significant influence on the education of the young and old in this nation. Surely they would also be recognized as professional educators.

If teaching is indeed to stand as a profession worthy of public support and confidence, changes on many levels will be required. Educators will need to hold their legislators to task on educational matters; convince taxpayers that spending dollars on the schools of this nation is a wise and moral investment; restructure schools and their curricula to make them more inclusive; assist school administrators in creating environments that are supportive of both teaching and learning; and involve the community, parents, and students in all of these efforts. Most important, teachers must participate in these changes from start to finish, for teachers themselves are the common denominator in establishing teaching as a profession.

As educators modify school structures and instructional delivery, schools of education must simultaneously redesign teacher preparation programs to match and participate in these changes. This synchronization is made particularly challenging by the separation of curriculum from experiences that still characterizes schools and many teacher preparation programs.

The book is organized around the moral principles or dimensions that should serve as the foundation of the teaching profession and teacher education.[2] "These moral imperatives," John Goodlad suggests, "arise out of the school's responsibility for enculturating the young, the necessity for and challenge of providing access to knowledge for all students, the unique relationship between the teacher and the taught in the context of compulsory schooling, and the role of teachers in renewing school settings."[3]

This book connects these principles of the teaching profession to both the preparation of new teachers and the nurturance of those in the existing teaching force. We argue that there is an overwhelming need to link the preparation of future teachers to the renewal of schools and of institutions of higher education. Throughout the book, we stress that teachers must care about students and the teaching profession, work hard, and continuously question their own professional values. We provide real-life examples of future and practicing teachers who are professional in their work. These examples come from data we gathered systematically from 1992 to 1998: more than three hundred pages of transcriptions of individual and group interviews of students and teachers, selected journal entries by students, internship summaries and descriptions, students' analyses of critical incidents in their classroom or school, portfolio entries, statements of philosophy about students with disabilities, intern inquiry projects, and our own field notes. We hope that these examples will make reading this book a personal and informative experience.

Chapter One begins with a discussion of the struggles facing democratic societies in defining and advancing professions and professional behavior. It then examines the varied definitions and conceptions of the terms *profession* and *professional,* with specific emphasis on the differences between a profession that fixes problems and one that enables change. This chapter suggests one possible future for the teaching profession, a future built on a moral base, and explores educators' moral and ethical responsibilities. The moral dimensions of teaching that Goodlad and his colleagues espouse are described along with other philosophical views on the topic. A consideration of the work of the teacher as ethical decision maker and as reflective and analytical professional rounds out the first chapter. The themes presented in Chapter One are woven throughout the rest of the book.

The second chapter examines the need for inquiry and reflection in the teaching profession. Inquiry and reflection are central to much of what follows: without reflective professionals, teaching has little hope of becoming an enabling profession. If teachers and their leaders are to arrive at solutions to current and future educational dilemmas, then inquiry is essential, and all parties (teachers, administrators, university faculty, parents, and students) must be involved. These inquiries must be responsible ones grounded in moral questions about learning, diversity, and the furthering of democratic principles. This chapter concludes with a consideration of the relationship between teacher evaluation and a teacher's ability and propensity to be reflective and inquiring.

In Chapter Three we detail the elements that must be present in a teacher education program that prepares competent, inquiring, and caring professionals who both understand and practice the moral dimensions of teaching. Advocating and creating a cohesive program that has a common purpose for preparing professional educators are put in the context of the struggles faced in doing so.

Chapter Four discusses the need for educative communities and professional development centers in the preparation and renewal of teachers. We believe strongly that making connections to our nation's schools and their surrounding communities is essential if institutions of higher education are to be an integral part of the teaching profession. The chapter delves into the concept of the "educative community"—both as it has been used in the literature and as we have come to understand it within the context of university-school-community partnerships. Overlapping notions of community are explored relative to the social context of schooling, and the strategy of working and learning in cohort groups is put forth as one form of community. The chapter then moves to a more specific discussion of the role of partnerships in the preparation of new teachers and in the renewal of schools.

In Chapter Five we emphasize that today's and tomorrow's teachers have a responsibility to a diverse population of learners. We make the case that the preparation of professional educators must be grounded in a philosophy that incorporates equity and diversity as central themes. This emphasis must be deliberate and practiced not in just one course but throughout a preparation program. Further, the relationship between diversity and equity in education, and the consequent access to knowledge for all, must be explored in many ways. The chapter suggests course work, clinical experiences, and readings that can be used to address the diverse nature of today's school population. Issues such as the inclusion of special education students in general education classrooms, language diversity, gender equity, and multiculturalism in school and society are offered as necessary topics for study and conversation among those preparing to be teachers as well as those already engaged in the profession.

Chapter Six posits that resistance to change is inevitable and that dissent is both necessary and unavoidable. Those who undertake reform of any nature will certainly encounter opposition. Preparing school professionals in a tradition of inquiry and reflection is therefore crucial. In this chapter we discuss the kinds of resistance that continue to influence professional practice, examining the teaching profession and its stewardship of change in classrooms, schools, and communities. The professional educator designs and implements organizational and curricular change within this context, and issues of pedagogy and nurturing are clearly linked. As schools change and as teachers become more professional, the educators' collective role as stewards will take on new clothing. This chapter projects what this new attire will look like. In many ways the chapter pulls together the contents of the previous ones and gives them a practical cast. It again stresses simultaneous renewal as essential to changing the profession. It reiterates the need for the moral dimensions as a framework for change in the teaching profession, drawing direct links between these moral imperatives and classroom practice. Finally, in closing this chapter and the book, we view the future of teaching through the stories of four professional educators. These accounts put the moral dimensions of teaching into action.

1

Teaching as a Profession in a Democracy
Creating a New Picture

The notion of a profession in a democracy is always evolving. Although sometimes the concept appears to be fixed, each profession or aspiring profession typically moves through successive approximations of the ideal over many years. In the case of the evolving profession called teaching, educators continue to struggle to find their way, to balance competence with moral responsibilities, and to believe that they can educate all children. Together, as Fenstermacher suggests, educators are painting a new picture:

> The picture [of teaching] is of a profession quite different from those with which we are familiar. It is a popular profession in that its practice is open to all who wish to struggle to achieve its ideals and master its requirements for competent practice. It is an egalitarian profession in that its practitioners use expertise and specialization not as instruments of status and control but as a shared resource of the group. It is a demanding profession in that it requires the reflective exercise of knowledge and skill, while being intensely engaged in the complex, perhaps greatly disadvantaged lives of one's students. It is—must be—a profession different from any of which we are immediately aware. To think of teaching in this way is to think of it as a fundamentally moral undertaking.[1]

Classical Notions of Professions

Most professions began as services performed by individuals within communities, usually part time. Gradually practitioners acquired more skill and knowledge through experience, and eventually the service became a full-time occupation. Apprenticeships were the common means by which to learn the skills and knowledge necessary to perform the service. In other words, trial and error shaped the developmental process.[2] As a profession develops, a commitment to learning more about the persistent problems or unknowns forms an ethos of inquiry. This, in turn, necessitates more organized forms of preparation that take longer to complete, and eventually professional preparation becomes a combination of university education and apprenticeship.[3]

Throughout this evolution, continuous debates occur regarding the profession's knowledge base, standards of practice, testing, licensing, and ethics. Usually an ongoing tension persists between the different epistemologies of professors and practitioners. Thus, the development of any profession is an untidy process. It has been no different for the evolution of teaching and the teacher's role in schooling.[4]

During the evolutionary development of teaching, we have come to formulate definitions of what the teaching profession is or should be. William M. Sullivan, for example, writes: "Professions are typically described as occupations characterized by three features: specialized training in a field of codified knowledge usually acquired by formal education and apprenticeship, public recognition of a certain autonomy on the part of the community of practitioners to regulate their own standards of practice, and a commitment to provide service to the public which goes beyond the economic welfare of the practitioners."[5] We would agree with Hugh Sockett who, in completing Sullivan's description of the essential features of the profession, held that an ethos of inquiry and moral agency must be part of any definition of the teaching profession. He tells us that "moral agency is nothing very fancy—simply, that a person considers the interests of others, does not make discriminations on irrelevant grounds, and has a clear set of principles or virtues in which he or she believes and on which he or she acts."[6]

These attributes of professional behavior are derived mainly from the histories of medicine and law. Over time, other professions have sought to emulate those leaders, but they have not always enjoyed complete success. Teaching, social work, and nursing, for example, have been called "semi-professions" because they lack such attributes of the recognized professions as the ability to exercise discretionary judgment and to control their own memberships rather than being under the sway of organizations that intentionally limit independent practice.[7] These very concerns are now forcing themselves on medicine and greatly challenging the practice of this profession.

Sullivan identifies "three constituent features of professionalism—(1) that professional skill is human capital that is (2) always dependent for its negotiability upon some collective enterprise which is itself (3) the outcome of civic politics in which the freedom of a group to organize for a specific purpose is balanced by the accountability of that group to other members of the civic community for the furtherance of publicly established goals and standards."[8] Here we find that professionalism is a matter of social trust, which is always precarious. Thus, as we witness the changes in health care, we see that what had seemed fixed is not as fixed as it had first appeared.

Professions in Nondemocratic States

In nondemocratic states, professionals are typically employees of the state, which directs the professions. In the case of teaching, the state determines the organizational, political, and ideological context of the profession: the educational system, the numbers and types of specialists trained, employment, conditions of practice, and salaries.[9]

Konrad H. Jarausch makes these observations about the role of German lawyers, teachers, and engineers between 1900 and 1950:

> The contribution of the professions to modern life has been profoundly ambiguous. On the one hand, the improvement of the legal system, the spread of learning, and the development of machines have increased justice, enlightenment, and comfort, thereby earning for professionals public gratitude and material rewards. On the other hand, the same experts have perpetrated callous injustice, engaged in stultifying indoctrination, and created engines of death for their own gratification and benefit. Hence critical observers have begun to question the social costs of professionalization: Are such recurrent abuses merely perversions of a positive ideal or are they inherent in the very nature of the professions?[10]

Jarausch chronicles that German teachers emerged from World War II with an updated version of the traditional educator-scholar-official role. Seeing themselves as guardians of embattled human culture, they demanded a university-trained teaching profession. "Their principal challenge," writes Jarausch, "was the 'cultivation' of character in a higher conception of humanity through 'absolute and historical spiritual-ethical values.'"[11] He notes that many professionals, because of their experience with the Third Reich, came to realize that "professionalism must be more than a selfish instrument for material gain. Only as an altruistic service to humanity, anchored in ethical commitment, and protected by basic civil rights, can professions make their full contribution to individual and collective welfare. Through largely self-inflicted disasters, some sobered survivors came to understand this essential connection between professionalism, social responsibility, and liberty."[12]

As professions develop, a critical variable is the knowledge base on which the work of the profession rests. Jones notes that this is cause for concern in socialistic societies: "Professions create a special problem for the party and state in socialist societies. For most theorists it is the knowledge base of an occupation that enables it to create the power that comes with professionalization. In socialist societies it is precisely this characteristic of an occupation that poses the most danger to the party's control of the society."[13]

But which lessons from socialistic societies apply to those that claim to be democratic? Elliott A. Krause observes that since World War II, professions in the United States have been facing the "growing power of the state and capitalist firms," whereas in Eastern Europe the professions have had "a slow increase in power, solidarity, and professional group autonomy" with respect to the state. He contends that in Western Europe, on the other hand, the power of the professions remains mostly unchanged in relation to that of the state. Krause also notes that since the 1960s, U.S. corporations have pressured the federal government to regulate professional work and the costs that professionals create.[14] More and more professionals in the United States are finding themselves in the role of paid employees.

It appears that past distinctions between professions in a non-democratic context and those in a democratic context are not as sharp as they once were. Nor is the definition of a profession as clear as it once was thought to be. Sullivan states that "the civic orientation in professionalism has been eclipsed by a more narrowly technical understanding, often to the detriment of professional life and the social compact which links professions to the larger society."[15]

Teaching and Teacher Education

Teaching has never been an occupation that lends itself to the classical definition of a profession. Teachers have been, by and large, employees. Because of their special charge—the education of the young to participate in a social and political democracy—they have always been under intense scrutiny, and their autonomy has been limited.

Teachers have recently been subjected to more and more regulation. Standards and testing dog them from the time they apply for admission to a preparation program until they retire. The rules of their work, always changing, allow little time for analysis of and reflection on their own practice or the knowledge they choose to impart to their pupils. Prescribed curricula and assessments have greatly curtailed their freedom to tailor curriculum and instruction to the needs and interests of individual children. States are attempting once more to "teacher-proof" schooling. What is happening is a far cry from what we find in the clarion call of John Goodlad: "a teaching profession grounded in the judgments that teachers in schools must make to maximize the education of all children and youths."[16] Similarly, Vivian Fueyo and Mark Koorland caution that "strong professional programs respond to knowledge production and scholarly norms rather than intuition and expediency. In strong professions, the arbiter of standards is the validation of research in practice, not the vagaries of the licensing agency."[17]

Yet, in the face of regulatory mandates, some of the important attributes of classical professionalism have characterized recent teacher education reform. Teacher preparation programs are paying greater attention to subject matter knowledge, general education, and pedagogical knowledge, in spite of external critics' continuing to treat these as either-or matters. In many cases, there is increased clinical preparation. Some colleges and universities have committed to partnerships with schools that serve diverse and poor student populations, thus reinvigorating the ethic of service that should undergird teaching and teacher education while simultaneously stimulating new and better teaching techniques. "Teaching as an ideal of service to developing persons," Sockett explains, "demands constant change and improvement if that service is to be properly pursued."[18]

Reflective practice and teacher research are beginning to be more widely incorporated into teacher education programs and teacher practice. A commitment to inquiry is imperative to improving practice and service and is therefore a central tenet of all professions. Sullivan comments that "reconceiving professional expertise according to the notion of reflective practice reveals the importance of experience and service to the professional enterprise."[19] There is a potential for conflict here between the ever-narrowing definitions of and standards for curriculum and instruction, and the teachers who are reflective practitioners dedicated to student needs and interests. Hargreaves and Goodson note,

> If teacher professionalism is to be understood as exercising reflective judgment, and developing and drawing on a wide repertoire of knowledge and skill, to meet goals of excellence and equity within relationships of caring then whether practical knowledge can provide a proper foundation for it depends on what that knowledge is, in what kinds of contexts it has been acquired, the purposes to which it is put, and the extent to which teachers review, renew and reflect on it.[20]

Sullivan's work on integrity and professionalism helps us here. He concludes,

> People are beginning to grasp with new intensity the objective need for responsible engagement and self-regulation. They are searching for ways to insure professional integrity, aware that it is a public good on which the welfare of all depends, but which cannot be ordered into existence simply by the manipulation of sanctions or rewards. Professional integrity is the outgrowth and legacy of the ethic of vocation. It can only be nurtured, given favorable institutional contexts, among free human agents who come to find an important part of their identity and meaning in the work they undertake.[21]

With all of this, we find ourselves asking the most basic yet at the same time complex question: How should teaching as an occupation be considered? Goodlad has long contended that "arguments for a profession of teaching in schools must arise out of the special layered context of the work, the complexity of this context, and the special knowledge, skills, and personal characteristics required for the burden of judgment entailed."[22] It is this very complexity that is ignored by many state departments of education, teacher evaluation systems, and members of the public. Real advances in teaching, learning, and teacher professionalism will require recognition of the inherent complexity of teaching and commitment to understanding and working with this complexity on a daily basis. Teachers, thinking and acting in professional ways, will find neither easy answers nor answers that work for all.

If this is the case, and it certainly seems to be, then the following summation by Goodlad provides the teaching profession with some guidance:

> The conditions necessary to legitimate self-proclamation of professional status include a thorough understanding of the role of education and schooling in a democratic society, an understanding of knowledge and ways of knowing that serve to interpret human experience, high-level competence in the special knowledge and skills required to educate the young in these ways of knowing, and substantial awareness of the standards of excellence and equity that must characterize schools and classrooms.[23]

As we move, then, to defining the profession of teaching, we must be fully aware, as Roger Soder argues, of the special context of teaching that makes it morally worthy to be classified as a profession. We cannot do this by comparing teaching to other professions, he states, but "teachers can legitimately argue for such worthiness because of the moral imperative that results from the nature of children and the nature of the relationship of the teacher, the parent, and the child. . . . The nature of the relationship is the reason that teaching is morally praiseworthy."[24] Gary Fenstermacher also ties the professionalization of teaching to the base of the profession, which is indeed a moral one:

> The rhetoric of the professionalization of teaching is grounded primarily in the knowledge base of teaching, not the moral base. Therefore, it is a rhetoric that clusters around notions pertinent to knowledge, such as expertise, skill, competence, objectivity, validity, and assessment. Yet . . . these are not the concepts that capture the essential meaning of teaching. Without the specification of the moral principles and purposes of teaching, the concept amounts to little more than a technical performance to no particular point.[25]

Indeed, recent commission reports and legislation, for the most part directed to technical competence, miss this point regarding the highly moral foundation on which the teaching profession rests. Committed, competent, and caring teachers need greater latitude for discretion to tackle the complex tasks they face every day of their careers. This latitude will be awarded only when the public and the profession itself willingly admit that teaching is inherently a moral undertaking.

The Moral Responsibilities of Professional Educators

> What we need in education is a genuine faith in the existence of moral principles which are capable of effective application. . . . We believe in moral laws and rules, to be sure, but they are in the air. They are something set off by themselves. They are so *very* "moral" that they have no working contact with the average affairs of

every-day life. These moral principles need to be brought down to the ground through their statement in social and in psychological terms. We need to see that moral principles are not arbitrary, that they are not "transcendental"; that the term "moral" does not designate a special region or portion of life. We need to translate the moral into the conditions and forces of our community life, and into the impulses and habits of the individual.[26]

John Goodlad and his colleagues have written extensively about what they call "the moral dimensions of teaching."[27] Goodlad also explicitly and compellingly argues that "the proper commitment [of teacher education] is essentially a moral one."[28] His focus on the moral nature of the teaching profession is not merely a rhetorical one. It is, we would suggest, a focus on the very heart of the educational process. Teaching, perhaps more than any other occupation, is profoundly and deeply concerned with issues of right and wrong, good and bad, appropriate and inappropriate. Indeed, a strong emphasis on morality has been at the core of the development of public schooling in the United States. Not only does society hold teachers accountable for their own ethical behavior as professionals but, even more, it expects teachers to serve as role models and exemplars for their students. Historically this meant that all aspects of teachers' lives came under public scrutiny, and teachers' contracts often explicitly articulated acceptable and unacceptable personal and professional behaviors. Further, there were widely shared social understandings of the kinds of conduct and behavior appropriate to teachers. Throughout much of American educational history, for instance, marriage meant the immediate end of a woman's teaching career; more recently, pregnancy had the same consequence.

Although few people would want American society and the teaching profession to return to the days when virtually all aspects of the private life of the teacher were deemed public, we do expect teachers' behavior to fall within certain bounds. The idea that teachers should serve as moral exemplars for their students retains its resonance in our society; it is precisely because of this expectation that we are so offended when an individual teacher violates the trust that has been given to him or her. There is, though, a significant difference in this regard between the past and the present, and that difference has to do with the lack of a common moral vision shared by the larger society. British philosopher of education Richard Peters explained in 1966:

> [Today] there are no set systems of teaching and no agreed aims of education; there is constant controversy about the curriculum and a welter of disagreement about how children ought to be treated. In more settled times only the very reflective teacher was led to probe behind tradition for a rationale of what he [or she] ought to do; nowadays it is only the lazy or the dogmatic teacher who can avoid such probing. Neither can the modern teacher find in the appeal to authority much more than a temporary resting place; for authorities disagree, and on what grounds is the advice of one rather than another to be heeded? The unpalatable truth is that the modern teacher has no alternative to thinking out these matters for himself [or herself]. Teachers can no longer be merely trained; they have also to be educated.[29]

We believe that educators have five distinct, although overlapping, types of moral responsibilities as part of their professional identity: to students, to parents, to society, to the institution, and to the education profession. Given the importance of these types of obligations for the professional educator, we turn our attention to the moral bases or dimensions of the profession, for in their practice they make possible the fulfillment of these obligations.

The Moral Dimensions of the Teaching Profession

> If one questions teachers about where and when they are
> called upon to resolve moral issues, they are likely to cite
> critical incidents involving the conduct of individual
> pupils and teachers; the moral principles underlying the
> teaching process itself are often taken for granted. Nev-
> ertheless, moral principles *are* embedded in practice; and
> it is because we believe teachers *ought* to recognize them,
> discuss them and evaluate them that we seek to include
> such activities in initial training courses.[30]

We agree with Michael Eraut that the requirements of the profession dictate that teachers recognize the moral principles inherent in their work. But what are these principles? How can they be
defined in ways that give dimensionality, and how might we encourage educators to discuss them often and openly? Their importance to advancing teaching as a profession is well documented, but
often disregarded.

A cogent, understandable, and practical definition of the moral
responsibilities of the professional educator must be articulated. Because teaching in a moral way asks the educator to be much more
than a good classroom teacher, we often revert back to a conception of teaching that is competency based. Although this view of
teachers' work is easier to define, it does not allow teachers to become
decision makers—about their classrooms or about their schools.
Strikingly few educators are knowledgeable about their moral responsibilities or willing to discuss them. Thus, definitions that lead
teachers to reflect deeply on these obligations must be put forth
often and with care.

In *Teachers for Our Nation's Schools*, John Goodlad provides a
framework for a conception of teaching that grounds the discussion
of the moral dimensions of teaching. To clarify the moral imperatives of the profession, he puts forth to educators their responsibilities to schools and children: "facilitating critical enculturation" of

the young into a social and political democracy, "providing access to knowledge" to all of our nation's children and youths in ways that are equitable, "building an effective teacher-student connection" through the practice of pedagogical nurturing, and "practicing good stewardship."[31]

To put it another way, Goodlad suggests that the moral considerations of schooling, and consequently the responsibilities of the teacher, are not simply separate pieces of the educator's work; rather, they are integral to all that the teacher does, both within the classroom and outside its walls. He tells us that moral considerations "pervade the whole, becoming moral imperatives for teaching, a profession of teaching, and teacher education. These moral imperatives arise out of the school's responsibility for enculturating the young, the necessity for and challenge of providing access to knowledge for all students, the unique relationship between the teacher and the taught in the context of compulsory schooling, and the role of teachers in renewing school settings."[32]

The work of Hugh Sockett adds another voice to the matter of the moral nature of the responsibilities and character of the professional educator. In *The Moral Base for Teacher Professionalism*, Sockett describes a "moral core of professionalism in teaching."[33] This moral core, he argues, is composed of "four primary dimensions in teacher professionalism: (1) the professional community, (2) professional expertise, (3) professional accountability, and (4) the profession's ideal of service."[34] With Goodlad's four moral imperatives, Sockett's moral core offers a definition of professional responsibility that is inherently moral: dedicated to service and community, to furthering our democracy through equitable education of the nation's young people, and to ensuring that the environment in which children are educated is a caring one. As Goodlad and Sockett make clear, "accountability" in a professional realm is much more than measuring teacher or student "standards." Landon Beyer juxtaposes the standards-driven, accountability position with the need for moral reasoning:

If moral reasoning is an inevitable part of human life, we might wonder why it has not always been central to the professional preparation of teachers. Several plausible reasons exist for this. First, a widespread understanding of professionalism in teaching has focused on the possession of specialized and typically isolated skills, techniques, and forms of knowledge to be acquired through teacher education programs and school experience. A decontextualized, technical approach to learning, classroom management, student achievement, teacher competency, standards-driven instruction, and the like implies that reflections on the moral significance of teachers' actions are unimportant aspects of school practice.[35]

The Ethical Obligations of the Teacher

"*Professionalism* describes the quality of practice," contends Sockett. "It describes the manner of conduct within an occupation, how members integrate their obligations with their knowledge and skill in a context of collegiality and contractual and ethical relations with clients."[36] Considerations of morality are not, of course, the exclusive province or responsibility of educators; issues of ethics and morals are of concern to all of us. As Stephen Toulmin has argued, "Ethics is everybody's concern. Scientific problems and scientific theories may from time to time intrigue or arrest all of us, but they are of immediate, practical importance to only a few. Everyone, on the other hand, is faced with moral problems—problems about which, after more or less reflection, a decision must be reached. So everybody talks about values."[37]

As a virtue of his or her profession, however, the educator takes on special responsibilities with respect to issues of morality. The National Education Association's (NEA) Code of Ethics of the Education Profession asserts in its Preamble: "The educator, believing in the worth and dignity of each human being, recognizes the supreme importance of the pursuit of truth, devotion to excellence, and the nurture of democratic principles. Essential to these goals is the protection of freedom to learn and to teach and the guarantee of equal educational opportunity for all. The educator accepts the responsibility to adhere to the highest ethical standards."[38] The educator's ethical obligations to his or her students are in many ways central to the moral nature of the education profession. Indeed, in the NEA Code of Ethics, the first principle emphasizes the teacher's "commitment to the student," which includes a number of explicit obligations that the teacher has toward his or her students. Specifically, the educator

1. Shall not unreasonably restrain the student from independent action in the pursuit of learning.
2. Shall not unreasonably deny the student's access to varying points of view.
3. Shall not deliberately suppress or distort subject matter relevant to the student's progress.
4. Shall make reasonable effort to protect the student from conditions harmful to learning or to health and safety.
5. Shall not intentionally expose the student to embarrassment or disparagement.
6. Shall not on the basis of race, color, creed, sex, national origin, marital status, political or religious beliefs, family, social or cultural background, or sexual orientation, unfairly—
   a. Exclude any student from participation in any program
   b. Deny benefits to any student
   c. Grant any advantage to any student.
7. Shall not use professional relationships with students for private advantage.
8. Shall not disclose information about students obtained in the course of professional service unless disclosure serves a compelling professional purpose or is required by law.[39]

This is a thoughtful list of the teacher's obligations to students. One of the more interesting and unfortunate characteristics of this list is that it must be understood to be a prescriptive guide rather than a description of common practice. In fact, it is all too common to find many of these ethical obligations routinely violated in contemporary American schools. One possible explanation for this violation is the general lack of moral consideration given to teacher decision making.

Teacher Decision Making from a Moral Base

During the course of a day, an educator makes hundreds, if not thousands, of decisions, many of them ethical in nature. Our concern here is with the quality of those decisions, because decisions about ethical matters, like decisions about any sort of matter, can be evaluated. In other words, some decision making about ethical issues is better than other decision making about ethical issues. This concept is obvious in a sense, yet difficult for some people to understand. As an example of what we mean here, John Brubacher, Charles Case, and Timothy Reagan tell the following story of ethics, decision making, and the "expert":

> A very common view today voiced by educators and others in our society is that all opinions are of equal weight, are equally valid, and should be equally respected. Such a view is certainly tolerant and no doubt well intentioned, but it is also, plain and simply, wrong. If you think about this claim in the context of medicine, for instance, you will see how absurd it really is. If I am suffering from a particular illness, my grandmother, the mechanic who services my car, and my physician may well all have opinions both about what ails me and about what should be done about the ailment. While I love my grandmother dearly, and while I both respect and trust my mechanic, on medical matters it would not seem to

be at all reasonable for me to trust either of them instead of, or in place of, my physician. Now, this does not mean that in a particular case one of them might not be more correct than the physician—but the odds (as well as human reason) would still suggest that I am better off to go with the expert. . . . The same, of course, would apply to the building of a house, the repair of a car, or the best way to teach a particular topic in the classroom. In each instance, some individuals will have greater expertise, competence, and skill than will others, and it is only reasonable and appropriate to favor their opinions somewhat disproportionately. This does not mean that once we have identified the experts in a particular field, we automatically empower them to make decisions. The actual responsibility for the decision making rests with us; it is my health, my car, and my house about which I must make decisions.[40]

When we turn to the area of ethical decisions and decision making, the problem is in locating the "experts." And in the case of teaching, affording teachers the opportunities to become experts through inquiry and practice is crucial. As John Dewey explains:

Inquiry, indeed, is a work which devolves upon experts. But their expertness is not shown in framing and executing policies, but in discovering and making known the facts upon which the former depend. They are technical experts in the sense that scientific investigators and artists manifest *expertise*. It is not necessary that the many should have the knowledge and skill to carry on the needed investigations; what is required is that they have the ability to judge of the bearing of the knowledge supplied by others upon common concerns.[41]

Inevitably ethical decision making, based on investigation, is a necessary part of teaching. Classroom teachers must recognize that judgments that are moral in nature are not merely matters of personal opinion or preference; they are, rather, positions, views, or practices that must be publicly defensible and supportable. Further, it is important to keep in mind that there is an important difference in some cases between what the institutional rules and regulations (or even laws themselves) dictate and what we may believe to be ethically or morally correct. And this certainly will be cause for personal conflict, thrusting on the teacher further dilemmas for reflection.

Education is an endeavor that is intrinsically moral in nature, and just as we wish to ensure that educators are masters of their subject matter, of the pedagogical knowledge of their craft, and of the actual methods to be used in the classroom, so too should we hope that they will be moral decision makers. Underlying all of these hopes is the goal of making all teachers reflective, inquiring practitioners.

Cultivating Reflective Practice and Inquiry

Reflective thinking is always more or less troublesome because it involves overcoming the inertia that inclines one to accept suggestions at their face value; it involves willingness to endure a condition of mental unrest and disturbance. Reflective thinking, in short, means judgment suspended during further inquiry; and suspense is likely to be somewhat painful. . . . To maintain the state of doubt and to carry on systematic and protracted inquiry—these are the essentials of thinking.[1]

John Dewey

The Nature of Reflective Practice

The phrase *reflective practice* has become ubiquitous in the literature of teacher education, and not surprisingly, a growing number of teacher preparation programs have explicitly committed themselves to preparing teachers who will be "reflective practitioners." Indeed, although not all teacher preparation programs have an articulated commitment to reflective practice, it would nonetheless be unusual to find a teacher preparation program anywhere in the United States that was on record as rejecting the goal of reflective practice for classroom teachers and teachers-to-be. Reflective practice as a goal of teacher preparation programs, in short, has become very much like "loving children" for many teacher education students and faculty—a slogan with a very high positive connotation and relatively little commonly agreed-on descriptive meaning.[2]

At the heart of our conception of reflective practice is the work of John Dewey, who wrote about the need for reflective thinking as early as 1903 and dealt with the role of reflection extensively in both *How We Think* (1910, revised 1933) and *Logic: The Theory of Inquiry* (1938). For Dewey, logical analysis was basically the generalization (in a systematic form) of the reflective process in which all of us engage on occasion. Dewey recognized that we can "reflect" on a whole host of things in the sense of merely "thinking about" them; however, logical or *analytic* reflection (the sort of reflection with which we are concerned here) can take place only when there is a real problem to be solved. Dewey saw true reflective practice as taking place only when the individual faces a real problem that he or she needs to resolve and then seeks to resolve that problem in a rational manner. The classroom is an obvious setting for such problems to arise, for both the teacher and the students. When problems occur for students, we have what is commonly known as a "teachable moment"; when they occur for the teacher, he or she is presented with an opportunity for meaningful reflection.

Teacher Decision Making

Much of the daily work of classroom teachers involves the making of judgments and decisions, often (indeed, almost always) with limited and hence necessarily insufficient information. In fact, teaching can be quite accurately and usefully conceptualized in terms of the role of the teacher as decision maker. Consider for a moment the many different kinds of judgments and decisions that the typical teacher engages in during his or her normal daily routine: curricular decisions, methodological decisions, decisions about classroom management and organization, decisions about both personal and professional ethics, and decisions about individual children—their needs and their problems. Philosopher of education Robert Fitzgibbons has suggested that all teachers make decisions of three types (which may and do, of course, overlap to some degree): those concerned basically with *educational outcomes* (that is, with what the goals or results of the educational experience should be), those concerned with the *matter of education* (that is, with what is, could be, or should be taught), and those concerned with the *manner of education* (that is, with how teaching should take place).[3] (See Table 2.1.) When a teacher makes decisions, he or she is doing far more than merely taking a course of action or acting in a certain way; he or she is engaged in a rational, intellectual activity. When we say that the process of decision making is a rational one, we suggest that the teacher (consciously or unconsciously) in fact engages in such activities as considering and weighing alternatives, in essence employing criteria to select an option or course of action. Unfortunately, as Jere Brophy has observed, "most studies of teachers' interactive decision-making portray it as more reactive than reflective, more intuitive than rational, and more routinized than conscious."[4] Good teaching, however, inevitably entails reflective, rational, and conscious decision making. An important facet of this process is that the teacher must be able to justify his or her decisions and actions in the classroom. This only makes sense, since justification of decisions and actions, as Cornel Hamm explains, is actually fairly simple and straightforward: "To provide a justification for a course of action is to provide good reasons or grounds for that course of action."[5]

In order to be able to provide such justification, the teacher cannot rely on either instinct alone or some prepackaged set of techniques. Instead, the teacher must think about what is taking place, what the options are, and so on, in a critical and analytical way. In other words, the teacher must engage in *critical reflection* about his or her practice. As one future educator told us:

Table 2.1.   Examples of Types of Teacher Decisions

Type of Teacher Decision	Nature of Decision	Classroom Examples
Educational outcomes	Concerned with the goals and/or results of the educational experience, whether measured or unmeasured, and whether long term or short term	Identifying learning outcomes and behavioral objectives, discussing "life outcomes" for specific components of the curriculum
Matter of education	Concerned with what is taught—the curriculum, both formal and informal	Recent debates about multicultural education and the development of more gender-sensitive and culturally diverse curricula
Manner of education	Concerned with the educational process— how students are taught—and what kinds of pedagogical approaches are appropriate and inappropriate	Teaching strategies and approaches, such as that manifested in the debate between advocates of whole language and more traditional approaches to the teaching of reading

Source: Adapted from Robert Fitzgibbons, *Making Educational Decisions: An Introduction to Philosophy of Education* (New York: Harcourt Brace Jovanovich, 1981), pp. 13–14.

Reflective practice to me is looking at situations that I encounter retrospectively, looking at things that I did to counteract a situation or how I behaved in the situation. Primarily, this means looking at myself and how I responded to a situation and figuring out whether or not there was a better way that I could have handled a situ-

ation. "What could I have done differently?" is the question I ask myself, in my quiet time, reflecting on what I
did so that if a similar situation was ever to occur again,
I would handle it better.[6]

This concern with reflection as part of teacher decision making
is hardly new. More than a quarter-century ago, Charles E. Silberman argued in *Crisis in the Classroom* that "we must find ways of
stimulating public school teachers . . . to think about what they are
doing and why they are doing it."[7] Teachers of the sort Silberman
desired are, by whatever name, essentially reflective practitioners.
Mark Van Doren perceptively argued,

Good teachers have always been and will always be, and
there are good teachers now. The necessity henceforth
is that fewer of them be accidents. The area of accident
is reduced when there is a design which includes the education of teachers. Not the training—a contemporary
term that suggests lubricating oil and precision parts, not
to say reflexes and responses.[8]

An important characteristic of the reflective practitioner is that
he or she is far more likely than nonreflective colleagues to demonstrate an awareness of and concern with what Thomas Green has
called the "conscience of craft." In a discussion of the formation in
contemporary society of individual conscience—that is, of moral
development—Green asserts that "there is such a thing as the conscience of craft. We see it," he continues, "whenever the expert or
the novice in any craft adopts the standards of that craft as his or
her own. In other words, it is displayed whenever we become judge
in our own case, saying that our performance is good or bad, skill-
ful, fitting, or the like. . . . Thus, to possess a conscience of craft is
to have acquired the capacity for self-congratulation or deep self-
satisfaction at something well done, shame at slovenly work, and
even embarrassment at carelessness."[9]

Recent Work on Reflective Practice

Recent emphasis on the need for reflective practice in education has been largely inspired by and grounded in the work of Donald Schön, which has been widely used by educators and others interested in the preparation of classroom teachers.[10] Such concerns with reflective practice are also tied closely to efforts to empower teachers, as Catherine Fosnot has noted: "An empowered teacher is a reflective decision maker who finds joy in learning and investigating the teaching/learning process—one who views learning as construction and teaching as a facilitating process to enhance and enrich development."[11]

A number of different ways of conceptualizing reflective practice as it applies to the activities of classroom teachers have been suggested in the literature. A good place to begin is with the distinction among the three types of reflection that Joellen P. Killion and Guy R. Todnem, using Schön's earlier work as a base, have proposed. According to Killion and Todnem, we can distinguish among "reflection-*on*-action," "reflection-*in*-action," and "reflection-*for*-action."[12] (See Figure 2.1.) Both reflection-in-action and reflection-on-action are essentially reactive in nature, being distinguished primarily by *when* reflection takes place—with reflection-in-action referring to reflection in the midst of practice and reflection-on-action referring to reflection that takes place after an event. Reflection-for-action, on the other hand, is "the desired outcome of both previous types of reflection. We undertake reflection, not so

Figure 2.1. Three Types of Reflective Practice

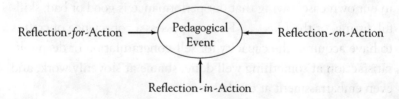

Reflection-*for*-Action ⟶ Pedagogical Event ⟵ Reflection-*on*-Action

Reflection-*in*-Action

much to revisit the past or to become aware of the metacognitive process one is experiencing (both noble reasons in themselves), but to guide future action (the more practical purpose)."[13] In other words, reflection-for-action is proactive in nature.

Clearly, all three types of reflection are necessary components of a classroom teacher's reflective practice. Nevertheless, the relative significance of each of these three components of reflective practice changes over the course of an individual teacher's career. For the novice teacher, reflection-for-action and reflection-on-action may be the most obvious ways in which his or her practice is distinguished; for the expert or master teacher, reflectivity may be best seen in reflection-in-action. Further, the process of engaging in reflection-for-action should be seen not as linear but as an ongoing spiral, in which each of the elements of reflective practice is constantly in motion in an interactive process of change and development. Finally, it is important to note that reflective practice involves what the teacher does *before* entering the classroom (in terms of planning and preparation, for instance), *while* in the classroom (both while functioning as an educator and in all of the other roles expected of the classroom teacher), and *after* he or she has left the classroom.

Max van Manen has suggested a hierarchy of "levels of reflectivity."[14] He contends that there are three levels of reflective practice that can be seen, at least ideally, as paralleling the growth of the individual teacher from novice to expert or master teacher. The first level is characterized by the effective and appropriate application of skills, materials, technical knowledge, and instructional strategies in the classroom setting. The second level of reflectivity involves reflection about the assumptions underlying specific classroom practices, as well as about the consequences of particular strategies, curricula, materials, and so on. At this second level of reflectivity, teachers begin to apply educational criteria to pedagogical practice in order to make independent, individual decisions about pedagogical matters. Finally, the third level of reflectivity (sometimes called critical reflection) entails the questioning of moral, ethical, and other types of normative criteria related directly and indirectly to the classroom. As Judith Irwin has explained, "This includes concern for justice, equity and the satisfaction of important human purposes within the larger social context. A teacher engaging in this level of reflection, then, would be able not only to make decisions that would be beneficial for the long-term development of the students in that classroom but also to contribute to educational policy beyond his or her individual classroom."[15]

Two future educators, the first preparing to teach in elementary school and the second preparing to be a high school English specialist, reflect on their experiences working in an inner-city high school and how these experiences have led them to reflect on the role of the teacher:

> I have developed greatly as a teacher and a person. Exposure to some of the problems that urban centers face brought me a better understanding of the challenges and roles that a teacher must assume in working with these students.[16]

> So much of this world tells the student that he or she cannot succeed or is not supposed to succeed. I doubt if I would have had such perseverance if I had to face the onslaught of negative expectations that many of these students face day in and day out. . . . So many things attempt to suppress the inner-city student. This internship has solidified [my understanding of] the need to give each student whatever is necessary in order to succeed.[17]

Another approach to conceptualizing reflective practice is to view such practice not in hierarchical terms but rather to focus on the elements that play significant roles in fostering reflection and reflective practice on the part of classroom teachers. Georgea

Sparks-Langer and Amy Colton, for instance, have argued that there are three such elements: the cognitive element, the critical element, and the narrative element.[18] The cognitive element of reflective thinking is concerned with the knowledge that teachers need in order to make sound and defensible decisions in and about the classroom situation. Lee Shulman has identified seven broad categories of knowledge that constitute the major categories of the knowledge base for a classroom teacher and that are therefore necessary for successful, reflective teaching practice:

- Content knowledge
- General pedagogical knowledge, with special reference to those broad principles and strategies of classroom management and organization that appear to transcend subject matter
- Curriculum knowledge, with particular grasp of the materials and programs that serve as "tools of the trade" for teachers
- Pedagogical content knowledge, that special amalgam of content and pedagogy that is uniquely the province of teachers, their own special form of professional understanding
- Knowledge of learners and their characteristics
- Knowledge of educational contexts, ranging from the workings of the group or classroom, the governance and financing of school districts, to the character of communities and cultures
- Knowledge of educational ends, purposes, and values, and their philosophical and historical grounds[19]

Although all teachers, novice and expert, have similar bodies of knowledge at their disposal, their organization and structuring of this knowledge may differ radically. Research conducted by cognitive psychologists has suggested that the schemata—organized networks of facts, concepts, generalizations, and experiences—of beginning and experienced teachers are different in significant ways.[20] It is in this respect—the ways in which experience and knowledge are organized—that the knowledge base of the experienced teacher can be said to be more expansive than that of the novice. Another way in which the knowledge base of the expert teacher differs from that of the novice is in the vast amount of tacit knowledge that he or she has accumulated and organized. As David Berliner notes,

> Experienced teachers amassed a large quantity of knowledge such that they did, in a sense, know their new class even before they got to meet them. This knowledge influences how subject matter will be considered, but is in fact an image or knowledge of classrooms that is a separate kind of knowledge. It is a knowledge that influences the running of the classroom: the pace, the level of intellectuality, affect, work orientation, and so forth. It is knowledge that influences classroom organization and management and is the basis for transforming subject matter. Such knowledge is complex, often tacit, derived from experience and worthy of being called expert knowledge.[21]

Teachers construct schemata for organizing knowledge over time as a result of their experiences, so it is not surprising that experienced teachers are often able to make sense of and respond to a problematic situation in the classroom more quickly and effectively than novices can. Studies suggesting that expert teachers are able to deal with changes in lesson plans and problematic classroom situations far more successfully than are new teachers can be explained, according to Sparks-Langer and Colton, "because (1) many of the routines and the content were available [to the expert teachers] in memory as automatic scripts and (2) their rich schemata allowed the experts to quickly consider cues in the environment and access appropriate strategies."[22] Schemata of the sort discussed here are constructed naturally over time, of course, but their development can be encouraged and supported by reflective practice. In other words, although good teaching practice does indeed depend to some extent on a strong experiential base, reflective practice can help speed up the development of such an experiential base in new teachers.

The second element of reflective thinking, according to Sparks-Langer and Colton, is the critical one that pertains to "the moral and ethical aspects of social compassion and justice."[23] Educators and educational theorists have discussed issues of social justice and ethics in education at least since Plato's time. Social justice and ethics are clearly manifested in such common and important distinctions educators make as that between educational product goals (that is, what they want to achieve in the classroom or the school) and process goals (that is, the restrictions that exist on how product goals can be achieved).[24]

The third element of reflective thinking that Sparks-Langer and Colton identified is that of the narrative voice of classroom teachers.[25] Teacher accounts of their own experiences in the classroom take many forms and serve a variety of different functions. Journals are one fairly common type of narrative. Other kinds of teacher narratives are descriptions of critical events in the classroom, various types of logs, conference reports completed jointly by teachers and supervisors or mentors, and self-interviewing. The key aspect of the narrative element of reflective thinking is that such narratives, whatever their form, serve to contextualize the classroom experience for the teacher and for others and thereby provide a much richer understanding of what takes place in the classroom and in the teacher's construction of reality than would otherwise be possible. Narrative accounts are becoming far more common, especially in the preparation of teachers and in qualitative research on class-room practices,[26] and there can be little doubt that they provide one of the most effective ways to encourage reflective practice.

One future educator discussed how writing and reflection go hand-in-hand for him:

> I've always been interested in writing, and so I've kept a journal. I think journals are a tremendous tool in terms of one's own growth. Writing, for me, is closely tied to my own growth, and I think that holds for teaching as well. Keeping a record of what you do, reflecting on what you do, and thinking reflectively about what you might do better is an important part of professional growth, especially in teaching.

He goes on to describe his aspiration to be a writer and how he will use journals in this endeavor:

> I think this will happen—my own avocation for writing—if I keep a personal journal that will mesh with my professional journal. That will be how I will go about trying to fulfill my aspiration. One of my favorite writers was Thoreau, and he wrote extensively in journals, millions of words. This was sort of his writer's workshop. I don't know if writers can write without writing a journal—it's a way of unpacking your thoughts.[27]

With this overview of the nature of reflective practice in mind, we turn now to a discussion of the ways in which the general concern with reflective practice has been developed and implemented in the University of Connecticut's Integrated Bachelor's/Master's teacher education program.

The University of Connecticut Experience

Although the phrase *reflective practice* has been defined in many different ways by many different educators, it has been used with a precise and clearly articulated meaning in the University of Connecticut context and is one of the most important threads holding together the theoretical foundations of the University of Connecticut's teacher education program. Our conception of reflective practice is tied to the current educational literature in a variety of ways, but is above all the product of the work of several key individuals on our faculty. They have spent considerable time and effort articulating what we mean by "reflective practice" as well as what the implications of this conception are for various aspects of teaching and teacher preparation.[28]

A teacher education program developed around the theme of reflective practice must start with a broad consensus about what exactly the term means and about how reflection of the sort desired will be manifested. After an extensive review of the relevant literature, a University of Connecticut faculty member produced a working document that was then used to promote discussion and debate among the faculty. Ultimately the following view of the reflective teacher was generally accepted by the faculty:

> A reflective/analytic teacher is one who makes teaching decisions on the basis of a conscious awareness and careful consideration of (1) the assumptions on which the decisions are based and (2) the technical, educational, and ethical consequences of those decisions. These decisions are made before, during and after teaching actions. In order to make these decisions, the reflective/analytic teacher must have an extensive knowledge of the content to be taught, pedagogical and theoretical options, characteristics of individual students, and the situational constraints in the classroom, school, and society in which he or she works.[29]

This description includes virtually all of the issues discussed thus far. We define the reflective teacher first and foremost as a decision maker who must make those decisions consciously and rationally.

Further, the reflective teacher must base decisions and judgments on a solid body of technical and content knowledge that is organized and reinterpreted according to his or her unique experiences. The reflective teacher must demonstrate ethical behavior and sensitivity as well as sociocultural awareness. As Charles Case, Judith Lanier, and Cecil Miskel have argued, "The attendant characteristics of professions include conditions of practice that allow professionals to apply this knowledge freely to the practical affairs of their occupation and to use their knowledge, judgment, and skill within the structures of the ethical code of the profession."[30]

Such a conceptualization of the reflective teacher makes clear how much is being expected of the classroom teacher by advocates of reflective practice in general and at the University of Connecticut in particular. This goal is not one that can be easily or quickly accomplished, nor is it particularly compatible with traditional models of teacher preparation. Indeed, in our view, much of traditional teacher preparation in the United States remains grounded, implicitly or explicitly, in what can be best described as an apprenticeship model of teaching. This model, whatever its benefits, is not appropriate for the development of reflective practitioners as we have chosen to define them.

The recognition that traditional approaches to teacher preparation would not suffice led us to the design of a radically new approach to teacher education, in which the concern for reflective practice would permeate virtually all aspects of a student's experience. The program links theory and practice in selected professional development centers, the extensive use of small seminars to provide students with opportunities to become increasingly reflective under the guidance of faculty members, the concomitant maintenance by all students of narrative journals intended to promote critical reflection, the undertaking of inquiry projects (generally of an action research nature) by all students in the final (internship) year of the program, and a series of related core modules in which the nature and purposes of reflective teaching, as well as the barriers to such teaching, are explicitly discussed. Perhaps most significant has been the willingness of faculty members to model reflective practice in their own teaching, encouraged by ongoing professional development meetings attended by faculty from all of the departments in the School of Education.

Inquiry and Reflection as Essential to the Art and Science of Teaching

There is a close and, indeed, necessary relationship between reflective practice and teacher inquiry. Such a claim presupposes that both reflective practice and teacher inquiry are worthwhile goals for professional educators—an assumption that is quite common among academics but somewhat less so, we suspect, in teachers' lounges. We are reminded in this regard of the comments with which D. C. Phillips began the preface to his book *Philosophy, Science, and Social Inquiry*:

> Woody Allen has written that unfortunately our politicians are either incompetent or corrupt, sometimes both on the same day. A parallel thought is often harbored about philosophers by their colleagues in academe—they are regarded as abstruse and irrelevant, and nearly always on the same occasions! There can be little doubt that some philosophers *are* abstruse, and no doubt the work of *some* is irrelevant. . . . But, as with many other complex fields, the arguments are easier to follow if pains have been taken to comprehend the *problems* or *issues* that are at stake.[31]

Although we would like to believe otherwise, our experience working with a wide variety of classroom teachers has made it clear to us that it is not merely philosophers who are seen as abstruse and irrelevant by teachers, but often academics in general. The goals of reflective practice and teacher inquiry are relevant to classroom practice and can be presented to teachers in ways that make this relevance clear. All too often, though, university-based educators fail to make such a case, and our rhetoric about reflection and inquiry falls on ears that we have bored to deafness. Our goal here is to make a case for the value of teacher inquiry as a necessary part of reflective practice that will be compelling for both classroom- and university-based educators.

At the heart of our concerns is the idea that the reflective practitioner must be not merely a consumer of knowledge but a producer of knowledge as well.[32] An important feature of the successful reflective practitioner will be his or her ongoing efforts to understand educational issues better, in both the classroom context and the broader social or community context. Thus, reflective practitioners inevitably engage in classroom-based inquiry, both formal and informal. As Dorene Ross, Elizabeth Bondy, and Diane Kyle have argued, "Reflective teachers are never satisfied that they have all the answers. By continually seeking new information, they constantly challenge their own practices and assumptions. In the process, new dilemmas surface and teachers initiate a new cycle of planning, acting, observing, and reflecting."[33] This need for teachers to seek out new information is connected to the proposition that teachers must be researchers. "Teacher research is very important," one teacher asserted, "because it maintains a dynamism of trying to find new and better ways of teaching and communicating. And I think this is more than passing on information; it is a way of teaching people to be self-sufficient. We have to teach people to teach themselves so that we can get out of the way and let them go in their own direction. That's my goal as a teacher. What I see is research and teaching going together as participatory research."[34] Further, not only is the reflective practitioner engaged in inquiry, but the nature of that inquiry should be classroom based and most likely of an action-research type, which James McKernan defines as "research by practitioners to solve their own problems and to improve practice. It is a growing form of professional development for the reflective practitioner."[35]

The Case for Teacher Inquiry in Reflective Practice

The world of educational research largely remains one of two opposing camps, each internally divided and suspicious of any heresies that might support the other. The ongoing debates about research design often focus far more on the specifics of methodological issues than on searching for answers to educational problems. Even more important in terms of the lack of utility of much educational research has been the lack of connection to and grounding in classroom practice. To be sure, the rhetoric in both the quantitative camp and the qualitative camp is far less strident now than has been the case in the past, and a growing number of researchers from both perspectives have called for more effective and meaningful dialogue between representatives of these two camps.

Indeed, a quick survey of much of the recent educational research literature would lead one to believe that virtually everyone involved in educational research is now agreed that the best research inevitably encompasses both qualitative and quantitative methods, techniques, and perspectives. Elliott Eisner and Alan Peshkin have suggested: "The camplike nature of the old quantitative-qualitative debate gradually is giving way to dialogue, so that the politics of method, while it persists throughout our universities, tends to resemble more the academic's ordinary concerns for turf maintenance than the bashing of illegitimate contenders by guardians of the faith."[36]

Such a view, however desirable, presents what must be conceded to be a somewhat optimistic picture of the relationship between quantitative and qualitative research, especially in the context of classroom-based research. Tensions do in fact remain, often related to discussions about what constitutes "research" and even "science."

We believe that it is essential that educators (university or school based) become more open to alternative understandings and conceptions of inquiry and research, and that this openness be reflected in their approaches to all aspects of the educational experience. Further, we believe that the model of reflective practice that has gained increasing credibility with respect to both the preparation of teachers and classroom practice can be usefully and productively applied to the practice of educational research.

Having said this, however, we believe that qualitative approaches to inquiry tend to be far more accommodating to the realities of the classroom than are more traditional, quantitative techniques. Among the most useful approaches to classroom-based research, in our experience, have been action research studies.

Action Research as a Vehicle for Teacher Decision Making

Although action research dates back to the 1930s in some disciplines, in the educational arena it is essentially a fairly new outgrowth of the qualitative research paradigm that has been gaining ground in recent years.[37] Robert Bogdan and Sari Knopp Biklen cogently summarized the premises of action research in the following way:

> Action research, like evaluation, policy, and pedagogical research, builds upon what is fundamental in the qualitative approach. It relies on people's own words, both to understand a social problem and to convince others to help remedy it. And, instead of accepting official, dominant, and commonly accepted understandings such as "schools educate" or "hospitals cure," it turns these phrases on end and makes them objects of study. Because the primary goals of applied research are action, training, and decision making, some differences from basic research exist.[38]

Action research is concerned with the development, implementation, and evaluation of solutions to real, immediate problems and concerns that classroom teachers face every day in their professional life. The source of the problem to be studied is experiential, the methods are pragmatic and flexible, and the goal is to promote positive change in a specific context. Action research is not, however, merely the application of "common sense" or even of the "scientific method" to classroom problems. Rather, it is a proactive, normative, and to some extent communal activity that requires and promotes reflective practice on the part of its practitioners.[39] Susan Lytle and Marilyn Cochran-Smith have suggested that such an approach to research inevitably involves epistemological and political differences from traditional practice: "As a way of knowing, then, teacher research has the potential to alter profoundly the cultures of teaching—how teachers work with their students toward a more critical and democratic pedagogy, how they build intellectual communities of colleagues who are both educators and activists, and how they position themselves in relationship to school administrators, policymakers, and university-based experts as agents of systemic change."[40]

Furthermore, action research provides a common meeting ground for school-based and university-based colleagues that is different in significant ways from the traditional experiences of both types of individuals.[41] Such a meeting ground, though difficult to achieve, is nonetheless valuable and worthwhile. "I have no illusions that . . . collaborative inquiry is a relatively easy and straightforward process," Kenneth Sirotnik wrote. "Those who have seriously invested their time and energy into activities of a related nature know well the difficulties of making collaborative concepts practical in less than collaborative settings. But many who have made the investment have considered it well worth the effort."[42] Finally, John W. Best and James V. Kahn have noted, "If most classroom teachers are to be involved in research activity, it will probably be in the area of action research. Modest studies may be conducted for the purpose of trying to improve local classroom practices. It is not likely that many teachers will have the time, resources, or technical background to engage in the more formal aspects of research activity."[43]

Perhaps most enticing for many practitioners is action research's emphasis on promoting change rather than on knowledge for its own sake or even on knowledge for purposes of generalization and prediction. Michael Patton has explained,

> Action research aims at solving specific problems within a program, organization, or community. Action research explicitly and purposefully becomes part of the change process by engaging the people in the program or organization in studying their own problems in order to solve those problems. . . . As a result, the distinction between research and action becomes quite blurred, and the research methods tend to be less systematic, more informal, and quite specific to the problem, people, and organization for which the research is undertaken.[44]

Although there have been and will undoubtedly continue to be questions raised in academe about the extent to which action research can be said to be "real" research activity, these questions are irrelevant; the process of engaging in action research clearly has benefits for those who engage in it, as well as for the classroom context in which it takes place. To the extent that it promotes reflective practice, school-university collaboration, the improvement of the teaching and learning environment, and teachers' discovering their own voices, action research is a valuable and worthwhile endeavor, regardless of its credibility or value as research in the academic world. As two classroom teacher-researchers put it: "For a long time, teachers have been charged with implementing theories developed by others. . . . Often excluded in the past, the voices of teachers and children are being welcomed as ones that can inform both theory and practice in unique ways. For it is teachers who spend their daily lives in the presence of children; teachers who are better placed than anyone to see what can happen when they begin to think differently about their work with children; teachers who can make change happen."[45]

The Role of Reflective Practice and Inquiry in Teacher Evaluation

Although the concept of reflective practice has been extensively discussed and debated in the teacher education literature in general, its implications for teacher evaluation have not yet been appropriately explored in any detail.[46] For the most part, where evaluation has been attempted, as in teacher preparation programs, it has tended to focus on qualitative measures, especially on journals and writing assignments. Dorene Ross has commented, "Teacher educators have turned to qualitative methods [because] reflective practice has yet to be defined clearly, and therefore quantitative assessment is precluded. In fact, because reflection is a mental process, as opposed to an observable behavior or set of behaviors, it may never be possible to develop a definition with enough behavioral specificity to measure it quantitatively."[47]

If reflective practice is to be taken seriously as a goal for classroom teachers, however, due regard must be paid to how it can be evaluated in the school context. Ross's claim to the contrary notwithstanding, if we are concerned with classroom practice (as surely we must be), then we must find ways of evaluating reflective practice that incorporate both qualitative and quantitative methods and perspectives.

Applying Dewey's theory of reflection to teacher evaluation calls for it to be redefined, as Kenneth Sirotnik does, as "the production of critical knowledge through the process of critical inquiry."[48] Such a view of the nature and purposes of teacher evaluation is quite different from traditional perspectives, of course, and may require a reconceptualization of the process and purposes of teacher evaluation. Consider the following statement from *The Personnel Evaluation Standards* of the Joint Committee on Standards for Educational Evaluation, which is intended to provide a compelling case for personnel evaluation: "The need for sound evaluation of education personnel is clear. In order to educate students effectively and to achieve other related goals, educational institutions must use evaluation to select, retain, and develop qualified personnel and to manage and facilitate their work."[49] Although the underlying point is that evaluation must facilitate professional growth and development, the rhetoric of the passage is somewhat problematic. The view of the role and purposes of teacher evaluation expressed in this passage is very common; indeed, it is without doubt the dominant view in contemporary American education. Although it is compatible with many views and models of teaching, and especially useful and appropriate for models that presuppose that good teaching is constituted by adherence to specific teaching competencies, such a description of the role and purpose of teacher evaluation stands in contradiction to a view of teaching that emphasizes reflective practice. For example, one of the central features of reflective practice is its emphasis on the need for classroom teachers to be empowered and enabled to construct, in large part, their own work environments. Rhetoric about evaluation's helping "to manage and facilitate their work," however well intentioned, is incompatible with such a conceptualization of teaching, because it not only debases the actions of teachers but also appears to presuppose a hierarchical relationship between teachers and administrators.

The teacher evaluation process may actually hinder a teacher's creative risk taking and self-reflection. As Johnson argues, this is largely the result of antithetical assessment and improvement processes in teaching.[50] Current assessment processes tend to foster caution among teachers, and real improvement in education depends on teachers' risk taking and critical self-examination. Further,

Johnson's work suggests that teachers are well aware of this polarity. One urban high school teacher, for instance, asserted that evaluation is "an absolutely worthless process, in my opinion, and I've said so publicly. . . . Evaluation allegedly is a tool to improve the quality of teaching. That's the avowed aim and goal of the evaluation process. In fact, I've never seen it either function that way or even be used that way. I've seen it used as an obligation: you have to be observed three times during the school year; that's the regulation."[51] Johnson found, in short, that teacher evaluation practices generally do not encourage teachers to improve or become reflective practitioners. An elementary school teacher sadly commented that even the so-called good evaluations left her questioning her competence: "I generally get an evaluation and it's 'Check, check, check—no problem. I don't need to come back to see you'—which is all right, you know. In a way it's nice, but in a way, I'm left thinking, 'I know I could do a lot better. I know here are things out there that I should be doing.'"[52]

For teachers to develop, to become risk takers and reflective practitioners, formative evaluation for improved performance must be separated from summative evaluation decisions that determine salary or job status.[53] As Johnson concluded, "When teachers feel threatened, they conceal their fears and their weaknesses, treating classroom observations as occasions for parading their strengths and teaching surefire lessons rather than venturing forth in new ways."[54] Such scripted theatrics can erode the collegial and cooperative relationship between teacher and observer and cause teacher evaluations to function as no more than a yearly obligation on the part of both parties.[55] Indeed, some researchers maintain that there exists "*no* clear evidence that teachers or administrators learn from evaluation."[56]

The historical problems preventing teacher evaluation practices from supporting reflective behavior on the part of teachers have been well documented. Administrators all too often develop evaluation criteria in the absence of teacher consultation or feedback.

Evaluation instruments fail to recognize the multidimensional nature and complexity of teaching practice and school contexts.[57] Edward Iwanicki, for instance, has argued that the mismatch between instrument and context is the result of a lack of clarity between teacher and administrator as to the purposes and goals of teacher evaluation: "Too often school systems become caught up in activities such as revising position descriptions, improving observation protocols, or simplifying evaluation forms, activities more related to how teachers are evaluated—when the real problem is a lack of common understanding between teachers and administrators as to the real purposes of the teacher-evaluation process."[58] School improvement should, in short, be a direct purpose of teacher evaluation.[59]

In a study of four school districts, Milbrey McLaughlin and R. Scott Pfeifer found that teacher evaluation based on school improvement efforts supported reflective teaching practice. This was the case because the outcome of an individual teacher's evaluation was interpreted dualistically, "in terms of the individual *and* in terms of the context in which the individual functions."[60] McLaughlin and Pfeifer suggest,

> Teacher evaluation conducted in an institutional context of mutual trust and support for evaluation thus initiates a cycle of reflection and self-evaluation at both the individual and institutional level. It not only provides feedback regarding individual and organizational effectiveness, but it also serves as an institutionalized trigger to stimulate routine reflection about the assumptions, norms, and values that support professional practice in a school district. . . . It is through learning of this sort that teacher evaluation stimulates a self-renewing process of problem-solving, action and reflection.[61]

An appropriate form of evaluation for classroom teachers striving to become reflective practitioners uses more qualitatively oriented evaluation strategies, techniques, and approaches.[62] A central feature of such qualitative evaluation is an emphasis not on standardized features of teaching behavior, but on the individual and contextual nature of professional decision making. It is essential that evaluators understand that practitioners do not merely take a body of cognitive information, techniques, and methodologies and apply them in a neutral, more-or-less predictable fashion in the classroom. Rather, the individual classroom teacher engages in the construction of his or her own reality, using as the basis for that reality teacher education content knowledge,[63] personal experience, intuition, and so on. In other words, qualitative evaluation of teachers must reject the overly simplistic view of the role of the teacher as an educational technician and adopt instead a view of the teacher as a professional functioning in a highly complex, individualistic, and often unpredictable working context.

To move toward assessment and evaluation procedures that are more appropriate for evaluating reflective practice will require peer evaluation procedures not unlike those used in the medical profession. In medicine, the practitioner is observed both formally and informally by more experienced members of the profession through direct observation and peer examination of selected cases on a regular review schedule. In addition, on a periodic basis, there will be a statistical examination of the results of certain treatments of various categories of disease or illness. If it is determined that an individual practitioner's success rates are falling, further investigation will be employed to try to pinpoint whether this indicates a problem and, if so, where the problem is, to allow for remediation. This approach to evaluation is collegial, collaborative, and field based, and it focuses on the improvement of practice. An important element of such an evaluative model is that it incorporates concerns about both the process of practice and the outcomes of practice— a dualistic approach with clear implications for education as well.

Let us apply the medical profession's type of evaluation to teaching. Competent peers, who themselves would be master teachers, would observe classroom practice and examine course materials, lesson plans, and evaluation instruments. The evaluators would ensure that the teacher performs his or her job in a professional manner and would offer the practitioner suggestions for improving practice. This assessment would be based not on tightly defined competencies but on collaborative commitment to broad areas of teaching competence such as those identified in the knowledge base of teaching proposed by Shulman. Presumably those areas of competence would include content, pedagogy, child development, and ethical behaviors. As is the case in medical evaluations, statistical analyses of school failure can illuminate sources of difficulty. Although student failure can be caused by a number of different factors—and the classroom teacher can in no reasonable way be held accountable for all of them—an ongoing high rate of student failure (however such failure is determined) is an indication of a potential problem and should be subjected to further examination. Such examination may, as in the case of medical practitioners, focus on areas in need of remediation and improvement on the part of the classroom teacher. Underlying such an evaluation process would be ongoing self-reflection as well, which is one of the ways in which the conceptualization of good teaching as reflective practice differs from most other models of teaching. In order to evaluate reflective practice effectively, different kinds of standards and criteria that are grounded in a more naturalistic and inquiry-centered approach to evaluation will be necessary.

3

Becoming a Teacher
The Moral Dimensions

Perhaps the very first question that the honest individ-
ual will ask himself, as he proposes to assume the
teacher's office, or to enter upon a preparation for it,
will be—"What manner of spirit am I of?" No
question can be more important. I would by no
means undervalue that degree of natural talent—of
mental power, which all justly consider so desirable in
the candidate for the teacher's office. But the true
spirit of the teacher,—a spirit that seeks not alone
pecuniary emolument, but desires to be in the highest
degree useful to those who are to be taught; a spirit
that elevates above every thing else the nature and ca-
pabilities of the human soul, and that trembles under
the responsibility of attempting to be its educator . . .
a spirit that earnestly inquires what is right, and that
dreads to do what is wrong; a spirit that can recognise
and reverence the handiwork of God in every child,
and that burns with the desire to be instrumental in
training it to the highest attainment of which it is ca-
pable,—such a spirit is the first thing to be sought by
the teacher, and without it the highest talent cannot
make him truly excellent in his profession.[1]

David P. Page, 1847

For most teachers, the initial path to becoming an educator was paved by their own history of schooling, influenced strongly by the teachers who taught them. As students, they learned to listen, take notes, and respond on multiple-choice exams. The teacher held the knowledge, and students were in school to learn it. The curriculum was set, and few teachers or students found ways to go beyond it. As a result, many of those who became teachers were steeped in the "way it should be," believing that the forty-five-minute period, the lecture format, and standardized curriculum and assessment were virtuous teaching techniques, if not aims of the educational enterprise. But as Dewey reminds us, "aims" are personal, not always bound to or dictated by educational organizations:

> It is well to remind ourselves that education as such has no aims. Only persons, parents, and teachers, etc., have aims, not an abstract idea like education. And consequently their purposes are indefinitely varied, differing with different children, changing as children grow and with the growth of experience on the part of the one who teaches. Even the most valid aims which can be put in words will, as words, do more harm than good unless one recognizes that they are not aims, but rather suggestions to educators as to how to observe, how to look ahead, and how to choose in liberating and directing the energies of the concrete situations in which they find themselves.[2]

Some people have been fortunate enough to gain insight beyond traditional approaches to teaching through a parent, grandparent, gifted teacher, or professional preparation program. These are the people who have both the intellect and the "spirit" described by David Page in 1847. A number of these individuals learned to inquire of the world around them and found, as a result of these inquiries, that there are few "truths" that hold for all. Some of these open-minded thinkers have become teachers and teacher educators who believe quite strongly that we will not advantage children to become citizens in a democracy without first educating teachers in a tradition of inquiry and understanding of others. Equitable access to knowledge for all can be achieved only through education that is grounded in a very different tradition of teaching: one that relies on teachers who are liberally educated; have the propensity for questioning, reflection, and action; and—most critical—have the capacity to nurture those in their care.

For these traditions to become widespread, teacher educators must design a curriculum that puts inquiry and reflection at its core, together with equity and diversity. This design must be coupled with an education in the liberal arts; teachers must themselves be well educated. Finally, this form of curriculum necessitates a wide variety of experiences with a diversity of learners. A curriculum constructed in such a way relies on the close, and indeed necessary, relationship among reflective practice, teacher inquiry, teacher education, and the renewal of schools as integrated missions in American education.[3] In this chapter, we describe the elements that must be present in a teacher education program that has the potential to prepare and nurture knowledgeable, competent, inquiring, and caring professionals.

This type of professional preparation is not possible in traditional teacher education programs that use apprenticeship models of "training," where programs of study are incoherent and splintered, a mission has not been articulated, and a broadly conceived moral education is not fundamental.[4] The socialization of teachers into the profession can be different when the schools and university share a vision and together clearly articulate a mission for the preparation of teachers. This collaborative mission of professional preparation must be grounded in the moral dimensions of the profession discussed in Chapter Two. John Goodlad has broken down the moral mission of teaching into four parts, each of which can be translated to state a moral mission for teacher preparation: preparing teachers who can help their students to become citizens in a democracy; preparing teachers who care—who nurture their students to learn; preparing teachers who will ensure that all children have access to the rich knowledge available throughout the world; and preparing teachers who are leaders and will serve as stewards of their classrooms, their schools, and their communities.[5] We are reminded here that the process of socialization into a profession espousing these norms is as important as the curriculum designed to prepare future teachers. Goodlad tells us that "socialization is a process of taking on certain cultural norms over time" and that "the socialization that occurs, formally and informally, in a teacher education program tells us a great deal about the images of teaching and the expectations for teachers guiding that program as norms. Such norms are apparent in both the explicit and the implicit curriculum."[6]

Teacher Education: Embedding the Moral Dimensions of the Profession

> Moral principles are real in the same sense in which other forces are real . . . they are inherent in community life, and in the working structure of the individual. If we can secure a genuine faith in this fact, we shall have secured the condition which alone is necessary to get from our educational system all the effectiveness there is in it. The teacher who operates in this faith will find every subject, every method of instruction, every incident of school life pregnant with moral possibility.[7]

In positing a mission for teacher education, John Goodlad suggests that four major curricular themes be considered and, further, that these "moral dimensions of teaching" should inform and guide the work of educators:

> Two of these components—enculturating the young in a social and political democracy and providing access to

the knowledge effective humans require—arise out of the educational functions assigned to our schools. The other two—teaching in a nurturing way and exercising moral stewardship of schools—are what teachers must do exceedingly well. Moral considerations give dimensionality and coherence to the whole; they are the substance of teacher education programs and the basis of a teaching profession.[8]

These moral aspects of the profession are important in developing teachers who understand democratic obligations, believe that knowledge should be available to all, care about young people and the schools, and are willing and able to assume positions of leadership. Embedding these considerations about the moral nature of the teaching profession should be central to designing a preparation program for future educators.

Preparing Teachers Who Will Help Students Become Citizens in a Democracy

To be a teacher in a democratic society carries a far greater moral responsibility than many prospective educators anticipate on entering the profession. All too often teachers view their work as subject or role specific, giving scant consideration to the place or importance of the curriculum they are responsible for in the larger educational enterprise. That is, they fail to understand that their teaching contributes to the education of future citizens to live and work in a democratic society. In his classic work, *Democracy and Education*, John Dewey reminds us of the responsibilities placed on education and educators in advancing a democratic society:

The devotion of democracy to education is a familiar fact. The superficial explanation is that a government resting upon popular suffrage cannot be successful unless those who elect and who obey their governors are educated. Since a democratic society repudiates the principle of external authority, it must find a substitute in voluntary disposition and interest; these can be created only by education. But there is a deeper explanation. A democracy is more than a form of government; it is primarily a mode of associated living, of conjoint communicated experience.[9]

Of critical concern here is how many future teachers have an understanding of the many meanings of democracy and its historical roots in this country. How many have read, as Roger Soder suggests that all teachers should read (among others), Plato's *Republic*, Alexis de Tocqueville's *Democracy in America*, George Washington's Farewell Address, Garry Wills's *Lincoln at Gettysburg: The Words That Remade America*, and Dewey's *Democracy and Education*? Further, how many future educators could have an informed discussion of the following lament by Robert Westbrook?

It may be, as Michael Walzer has gloomily suggested, that in modern societies citizenship is fated to wither in favor of the more passionate identities of class, ethnicity, religion, and family, which "do not draw people together but rather separate and divide them" and hence "make for the primacy of the private realm." But, to believe this is to guarantee the permanent eclipse of an expansive democratic citizenship. To imagine that American democracy can be reconstructed and revitalized requires, as John Dewey said, an abiding faith in the ability of ordinary men and women to educate themselves and their children for self-government and in their will to use the power at their disposal to wage the long struggle necessary to secure the means of self-government. Democrats of this neo-Jeffersonian sort must expect a torrent of criticism from neo-Hamiltonians who will charge that such a faith is unreasonable and even reckless, and they must be prepared for frustrations, setbacks, and many a long, dark night of the soul.[10]

We propose that students preparing to be teachers of our nation's future citizens should be quite able to participate in such a conversation. Here we mean teachers broadly speaking—not just those who would be history or social studies teachers—for it is the responsibility of all teachers to create educational environments that emulate democratic values and configurations. These values and configurations should be both implicit and made explicit to students. One of our teacher education students, a future mathematics educator, wrote this journal entry:

> Tonight [in a graduate course in education] we talked about what kinds of things are disempowering to our students. We came up with many ideas that fit the category. . . . As we talked about all of these, however, my mind began to wander, which is not uncommon. I thought about what kind of school system would be empowering. More specifically, I thought about what kinds of teachers would fill the halls (if there were halls). What immediately popped into my head was a group of people walking around in sandals and togas. I thought that in a utopian school system people like Plato and Socrates would be the educators. In a totally empowering school system, there would be no school or, for that matter, a system. . . . If the school system tended toward the "state," then I would be truly concerned for our nation's well being. . . . However, instead of trying to reach an unreachable goal that would not be consistent throughout our society, I believe that we should have goals that are more attainable.[11]

Fostering in Teachers a Dedication to Ensure That All Children Have Access to Rich Knowledge

Access to knowledge is more than the knowledge itself and more than the methods of instruction; it is also place conscious. In many of our nation's schools, equal access to knowledge is limited by an unequal distribution of resources, including human resources. Jonathan Kozol chronicles in *Savage Inequalities,*

> The problems are systemic: The number of teachers over 60 years of age in the Chicago system is twice that of the teachers under 30. The salary scale, too low to keep exciting, youthful teachers in the system, leads the city to rely on low-paid subs, who represent more than a quarter of Chicago's teaching force. . . .
>
> But even substitute teachers in Chicago are quite frequently in short supply. On an average morning in Chicago, 5,700 children in 190 classrooms come to school to find they have no teacher. The number of children who have no teachers on a given morning in Chicago's public schools is nearly twice the student population of New Trier High School in nearby Winnetka. . . .
>
> The shortage of teachers finds its parallel in a shortage of supplies. A chemistry teacher at the school reports that he does not have beakers, water, bunsen burners. He uses a popcorn popper as a substitute for a bunsen burner, and he cuts down plastic soda bottles to make laboratory dishes.[12]

John Goodlad considers these same matters of access to knowledge, pointing out that we have failed to be true to our rhetoric when it comes to the education of all children: "The inequitable handling of budget exigencies illustrates that we have not yet built into the civility of our culture educational beliefs, policies, and practices fully reflective of a rhetorical commitment to education for all. We have not as a nation matured to widespread understanding of the role of education in gaining full participation in the human conversation, not merely a job."[13]

Thus, programs that prepare future teachers must make a self-conscious effort to ensure that teachers have a richness of knowledge to impart to their students. But there must also be a strong commitment to preparing teachers who can and will teach effectively in environments where equal access is not a given—for example, in city schools or in rural areas. Teacher education programs must also enculturate future teachers to accept and work with diverse populations, such as students with language differences or disabilities. One future educator explains: "I believe that education should allow people to participate in American society to the best of their abilities. As a future educator, I support the legal provisions that support teaching and instruction designed to improve the education of all students."[14]

Access to knowledge is directly tied to the equal and appropriate access to resources for all students. As an example, many children and adults with disabilities still do not have equitable availability of inclusionary classrooms and schools. Certainly debates do take place over what is the most appropriate or "least restrictive" learning environment; nevertheless, teachers engaged in this debate should believe that the inclusion of students with disabilities in the general education classroom can and often should be the norm. A student preparing to be an elementary educator discusses this possibility: "Inclusion, when offered with the appropriate level of resources and help, is the ideal educational setting. For me, the inclusionary school is the last defense against a total loss of community spirit. Inside an inclusive classroom, equity is in its finest form. It offers an umbilical connection to a better society, and it is up to me and my contemporaries to further this vision."[15]

Developing Teachers' Capacity to Care and to Nurture Student Learning

Donna Kerr, in her enlightening work *Beyond Education: In Search of Nurture*, stresses the need for community, civility, and an intellectual life grounded in nurture. She concludes the essay with this call for action:

> We must come to understand that while institutions and their policies cannot nurture selves, they do have the power to render nurture virtually impossible. We urgently need public policy that will robustly encourage life in family and community. We desperately need to avail children of the adults in this society. And we can only hope that we, as adults many of whom understandably still struggle to find ourselves, will be willing and able to nurture our young and one another.[16]

Nurturing teachers are successful not only at imparting knowledge but at enabling children to learn for themselves, create their own knowledge, and care about themselves, their community, and their own learning. Such teachers practice pedagogical nurturing in every lesson, in every human interaction with others as well as with themselves. These are teachers who continue to learn and participate in the human conversation in order to nurture.

By pedagogical nurturing we mean that teachers impart to their students the wisdom of the past and the debates of the present, creating situations for students to generate their own problems, solutions, and knowledge. For this to happen, teachers must have something important to teach (that is, they must themselves be informed), they must have the capability to teach well what they know, and they must continually help children, through their example, to care about learning, themselves, and each other. Goodlad would call this process "building an effective teacher-student connection."[17]

In 1916 Dewey articulated the reciprocal relationship between teachers and learners in telling us that too often teachers do not reflect on either the engagement of students in the process of learning or on their own learning that results from their interactions with learners. He points out that educators tend to create classroom conditions under which neither they nor their students actually learn much:

We can and do supply ready-made "ideas" by the thousand; we do not usually take much pains to see that the one learning engages in significant situations where his own activities generate, support, and clinch ideas—that is, perceived meanings or connections. This does not mean that the teacher is to stand off and look on; the alternative to furnishing ready-made subject matter and listening to the accuracy with which it is reproduced is not quiescence, but participation, sharing, in an activity. In such shared activity, the teacher is a learner, and the learner is, without knowing it, a teacher—and upon the whole, the less consciousness there is, on either side, of either giving or receiving instruction, the better.[18]

A future mathematics educator, T. J. Kopcha, working in a graphics arts laboratory using technology as its major medium, describes his awareness of the reciprocal nature of the learning process:

> [As] I began my internship, I expected to create some lessons and take the students through those lessons. Much to my surprise (and delight), Pat's class does not run like a typical classroom. . . . The students are allowed to explore and experiment in areas that they choose. . . . I began to realize that I was not the typical teacher, nor was my role solely to teach. I was a learner just like my students were. "Hey mister," they would call out, "How do I do this?" "I don't know," I replied honestly. "But I know we can figure it out." . . . Imagine a mathematics classroom where the teacher learns with the student. Students will come to know that any problem can be solved with the right efforts.[19]

T. J. personifies what we understand pedagogical nurturing to be: he knows the subject matter, he nurtures his students to engage in their own learning, and as a result of the reciprocal relationship he has helped to create, he learns much. He has also done something more: cared for each of his students. The work of Nel Noddings is of particular relevance here. In her two seminal works, *Caring: A Feminine Approach to Ethics and Moral Education* (1984) and *The Challenge to Care in Schools: An Alternative Approach to Education* (1992), Noddings makes the strong and convincing case that the enterprise of teaching is about much more than knowledge. In both books she argues that caring is an essential and necessary condition not only to learning and schooling but to the moral and ethical connectedness of schooling and democracy. Caring is cut from many fabrics, and the teacher in a sense becomes the tailor—fashioning environments that are caring and that teach students to care for their learning and for one another. In the following passage, an intern speculates on how a change in his classroom arrangement (he added a number of students to a computer mathematics class for those with special education needs) affected his students' sense of pride in their work and in the creation of an environment that was one of caring:

> The students in my second period class are now quite comfortable with our new arrangement. They are able to get through more lessons in this manner and, I believe, are coming out with a deeper understanding of the material. What is truly wonderful is that the atmosphere in the classroom is one of caring. Some of the students have to share computers. This has actually been worthwhile because the students work with each other. Also, each student has different levels of motor skills, math skills, spelling skills, and thinking skills. . . . It's purely speculation, but maybe the students gain the respect of their peers by showing their strengths. Furthermore, some of the students have taken on the role of my assistant to their peers. One student is able to get the "hang" of the

lesson quickly and thus helps the others. Another student who has trouble will want to help. When I let her,
she feels a sense of accomplishment that really makes her
proud.[20]

As future teachers experiment in the creation of environments
that nurture, they will inevitably confront situations where others
in the profession do not care and do not take to heart the importance of the relationship between teachers and those in their care.
Teacher educators must be ready to help these future teachers deal
with situations such as the one described by an extremely intelligent,
caring, and reflective future English teacher and special educator:

Today a bright young man that I have developed a strong
personal connection with dropped out of school. The sad
thing is that he was a senior and that he was (in my
view) one of the school's better students. Even though
his grades may not reflect it, he was smart and able to do
high levels of critical thinking. He dropped out of school
because, "I don't deal with this b.s. anymore." To many
of the teachers and counselors, he was just another number and name. Upon discussion with several people involved with this young gentleman, these were some of
the comments I heard:

1. "If he drops out, it will make all our lives easier.
   He's one less kid I have to deal with."
2. "No great loss to me."
3. "He'll be dead within a year. I knew he was no
   good when I first saw him."
4. "Dropping out—Great!"

These comments not only appalled me, but they made
me ashamed that these people are to be in my "professional circle." The Little Prince said, "You have become

responsible forever for what you have tamed." This student and I have tamed each other. We developed a strong bond; however, it was not strong enough to help him through these *LAST* two months before graduation. I feel that we have all failed him—we did not get to know him and provide him with support to help him succeed in school.[21]

Although Jennifer Del Conte was not able to help this young man graduate from high school, her dedication to future students and to improving the system only strengthened as she gained experience. During her first year of teaching, her predilection to care led her to consider the importance of stewardship and its connection to the reciprocal relationships among student, teacher, and learning:

The kids that I work with keep me busy. They are a hard group to win over, but I've managed to establish a good rapport with them. Often they seek me outside of class to "chat." This is just as important as classroom stuff because the content is driven by the students. . . . Because they are deaf, they miss a lot of the extraneous information hearing people pick up every day. Many of my colleagues brush them off and clock the time they are "teachers." I believe that some of the best teaching happens outside of school! That's why it's important to be involved in activities, socials, etc. It is during these events that students see teachers as humans. Teaching is not a job that begins at 7:00 and ends at 3:00. Teaching is evolutionary and becomes a part of who you are as a person. Good teachers are "artists" and "scientists." They practice a craft—the sharing of knowledge.[22]

Inspiring Teachers to Lead and to Serve as Stewards

Goodlad suggests that our nation might reasonably expect that its teachers be "among the best-educated citizens" and that they hold a strong belief that all children can learn.[23] He goes further in holding teachers responsible for the stewardship of their classrooms, schools, and communities: "It is reasonable . . . to expect teachers to be responsible stewards of the schools in which they teach. They and they alone are in a position to make sure that programs and structures do not atrophy—that they evolve over time as a result of reflection, dialogue, actions, and continuing evaluation of actions. Teachers are to schools as gardeners are to gardens—tenders not only of the plants but of the soil in which they grow."[24]

For a teacher to become this type of educator—an educator such as Jennifer Del Conte—the program that he or she is prepared in must foster such attitudes and behaviors. A future English educator discusses how the type of education he is receiving will mobilize people to change the system: "The program has made us want more, and you need a population of educators who are more powerfully trained and who are really interested in changing the system. The program mobilizes a great number of people, together, who are going to be very educated and want to change the system."[25]

Recall T. J. Kopcha's words about the reciprocity of learning that transpires between a teacher and his or her pupils. His reflection continues here, connecting students' learning to the teacher's ability to change the nature of the classroom, work with colleagues, and in the process create a better environment for all to learn and grow in:

> When I began the internship, I never expected to change the classroom as much as I have. Pat defies the attitudes of most teachers his age. While his colleagues grow comfortable in daily routines and repeated lesson plans, Pat constantly looks for improvement. He wanted change in the classroom as badly as I did, and together we accomplished our goals and then some. When I picture myself teaching years from now, I see myself as a similar teacher. Change will be a necessary, welcome addition to the list of my goals.

I often hear people say, "Well, what we do works fine, so why try and change it?" After being in this internship, I have found an answer. . . . Because you can always make it work *better!* If you attempt change and it fails, you can always go back to whatever worked "fine." But imagine if you succeed, and your change makes the "something" work better. Is the risk of failure worth it? By all means yes! If there is one thing I learned about failure this year, it's that failure is the best source of knowledge. . . . If I am not afraid to fail, then the people around me will begin to feel the same way. The focus of change should not be the potential failure you may face. The focus should be on trying. If you give up on an idea before you've ever tried it, you fail before you ever begin. . . . Pat and I still want more for the classroom. He talks about writing more grants for better computers. I talk about connecting the room to the Internet and the World Wide Web. . . . Pat and I are, above and beyond being colleagues, good friends. . . . A final word about the internship. I entered the internship without any idea of what I could offer to the site. I not only discovered how to initiate change and teach, I discovered myself.[26]

Constructing a Program of Professional Preparation

Embedding the moral principles or dimensions of teaching into a teacher education program is easier said than done. All too often, programs preparing teachers have been constructed piece by piece, in a random fashion. A course is proposed and passed; a faculty member believes in one method of instruction, while another embraces a competing method; elementary educators are prepared separately from secondary teachers, and special educators are prepared in isolation of their future teaching partners. What transpires over time has little common purpose or recognizable coherence. "The problem," John Goodlad writes, "is that the necessary pieces and connections are walled off by institutional organizational arrangements. Moving highways from here to there and digging tunnels under cities are child's play compared to breaking down those walls and creating new, functional arrangements."[27] Those faculties attempting to "break down walls" in lieu of "digging tunnels" must first articulate a mission for teacher education in which the moral dimensions of teaching are central.

Espousing a Common Purpose or Mission

Prior to the construction of a sequence of study or course work, the faculty (including those in other parts of the university as well as those from schools working collaboratively in the arena of teacher preparation) must set out to articulate a common purpose or mission for the education of future teachers. Reaching understandings relative to the moral aspects of the profession will require deliberation on how reflection and inquiry, equity and diversity, school-university connections, admission in cohorts, the place of teacher education in the university, and the core of curriculum will be addressed.

Goodlad's *Teachers for Our Nation's Schools* provides guidance in this area. Some institutions have taken his and others' suggestions and have formulated statements of mission that in fact provide a foundation on which a coherent and morally grounded program can be built. One example of a statement of program mission or purpose is the description of its teacher education program sent by the University of Washington to prospective students (see Exhibit 3.1). The University of Washington teacher education faculty talk about much more than students' simply joining an excellent program. They describe their belief in "educating teachers for a democratic and inclusive society" and in "the development of ethical, caring teachers who understand their responsibility to educate all students." They alert potential students in their teacher education program to the full-time, intense nature of the program and to the professional standards and code of ethics that all who are engaged in the program must abide by.

**Exhibit 3.1. Program Statement for the Teacher
Education Program/Master in Teaching, University
of Washington College of Education**

From the Faculty:

Thank you for your interest in the University of Washington Master
in Teaching program leading to teacher certification. The faculty and
staff at the University of Washington and the faculties of our partner
schools and departments are committed to providing the highest quality
professional preparation program and to ensuring that all students will
continue to be educated by caring, dedicated, and competent teachers.

We believe that the process of educating teachers must value both
academic preparation grounded in the best available research, theory,
and practice and the immediate application of these concepts in real
situations. We, therefore, have established linkages between the College
of Education and the College of Arts and Sciences and cooperative
agreements between the University and the partner schools and
departments who will work with us to provide the best possible field
placements for all students.

We believe that the process of educating teachers must take into
consideration the prior knowledge, experiences, and beliefs of our adult
students. We will work from this foundation as students acquire the
knowledge and skills needed to become teachers.

Our program is based on several fundamental principles, which are
modeled in various forms throughout the course of study. We believe
that the process of educating teachers for a democratic and inclusive
society implies the responsibility for ensuring that our graduates have
high standards for both their own conduct and that of their students.
We are committed to the development of ethical, caring teachers who
understand their responsibility to educate all students and to believe in
each student's ability to learn and grow. Therefore, we have set forth
Professional Standards and a Code of Ethics for students and will require
all students and all people associated with the Teacher Education
Program to abide by that Code.

We believe that becoming a teacher is a lifelong learning process.
This program is one step in the process, other steps have preceded it,
and many more will follow. Therefore, we will encourage students to
engage in problem solving and professional exploration, to learn to

**Exhibit 3.1. Program Statement for the Teacher
Education Program/Master in Teaching, University
of Washington College of Education, cont'd**

collaborate and cooperate with peers in the program as well as with the
staffs of the schools in which they are placed, and to communicate with
colleagues throughout the country, and the world, through electronic
media and professional journals.

The program consists of an integrated sequence of daytime
coursework and field experiences emphasizing the application of best
practice and research. Major topics are the social contexts of teaching,
content area teaching, students' diverse needs, interdisciplinary
curriculum, technology for teaching, multicultural education, assessment
and evaluation. Field experiences are in partner schools, schools in the
Seattle/Puget Sound area chosen to provide a variety of situations with
regard to level, school population, and location. The culminating field
placement is a full-time fourth quarter teaching experience. Students
return to campus for a fifth quarter, during which they construct a
portfolio emphasizing professional reflection, evidence of learning from
the program, and professional development.

Because we believe that the sequencing of coursework and practical
experiences is essential to the development of a coherent program, we
require all students to attend full time throughout the program, taking
the coursework and associated field experiences within the time frame
provided by the program. It is, therefore, imperative that students
carefully plan time to accommodate assignments from both the field and
University campus.

We are proud of our program and would be glad to answer any
questions you might have about it.

Struggling with Practical Elements and Constraints

Any program working to create common understandings about the
mission of teacher education will face practical challenges unique
to its own institution as well as others that have historically characterized colleges and university structures. Here we do not address
all of these constraints but rather put forth a number of commonly

encountered barriers that can influence a faculty's ability to construct a coherent program of professional preparation.

First, the college or school of education, in concert with the institution, must decide who from the faculty will be involved in the teacher education program and to what degree. In making these decisions, both the faculty and the administration are influenced by issues pertaining to the definition of scholarship, reward structures, promotion, tenure, and the like. Ernest Boyer's *Scholarship Reconsidered* challenges academe to address these issues, but all too often history carries more weight than an up-to-date discussion of this barrier to change in the ways in which faculty typically view their work.[28] Thus, if faculty roles are to take new shape and direction, if work in teacher education and service to the broader educational community are to be appropriately valued, and if more of the faculty from within and across the institution are to participate, changes in the way research is conducted and evaluated, in how courses are taught, and in how faculty are granted promotion and tenure will be essential.

Although teacher educators across departmental lines and programs have begun to address their new roles in schools and academe, there continues to be an underlying tension among faculty who are traditionally wedded to their individual disciplines. In some cases, this is expressed in terms of the research responsibilities in a university setting; in others, it is about the time that working with schools takes. Put still another way, some faculty members worry that an integrated teacher preparation program might take away from the specialization of each teaching discipline. Collaboration is difficult, but if we expect school teachers to work together, we should expect those in higher education to do the same. Yet entrenched ways of thinking about one's job permeate both environments. As an example, team teaching has proved to be both successful and rewarding in schools and at the university, but this configuration of professional time does not fit easily into scheduling and teaching loads.

The next concern, or possibly the place to start, is with the problems that an academic unit that prepares teachers typically faces in finding a home for the teacher education program. Will this home be the entire college or school of education or a subset of the college? How will others from inside and outside the college or university find a room in this home? Goodlad proposes that this home be a "Center of Pedagogy"—a place where those committed to the education of educators and to renewing America's schools can interact on common matters.[29] He suggests that the three major residents of this home be faculties from the arts and sciences, the school or college of education, and partnership schools. Bringing these groups together gives strength to the mission of teacher education and fosters inquiry—about the setting's own teacher preparation program, about teaching and learning, and about "the needs and characteristics of [the] public context."[30]

The influence and intrusion of the state often pose other barriers to change. Changes in certification regulations set forth by state departments of education often come with little or no input from institutions preparing educators. These regulations—about how teachers should be certified and consequently classified to do one job or another—do not always match the best judgments of the professional literature or thought. State departments should be allies of educators in teacher preparation, but sometimes they are quite the opposite. The influences—or sometimes random intrusions—by outside constituencies are often confounded or exacerbated by the lack of continuity of leadership.

The Curriculum of Professional Preparation

Once a mission has been agreed on and contributing members have, at a minimum, consented to work with one another toward fulfilling that mission, the essential elements of the program are identified. A number of key characteristics should be inherent in a curriculum of professional preparation. This curriculum would prepare teachers who would consequently have the knowledge and propensity to act and think in professionally moral ways. Curriculum characteristics or components would not seek simply to comply with competencies or standards but would move beyond compliance to incorporate teaching competence into a professional culture that is intellectual, reflective, and morally grounded.

Like fibers twisted together into thread or rope, "strands" of professional preparation—specific course work, fieldwork, and other experiences—combine to form a total curriculum of professional preparation that has coherence. Figure 3.1 provides a graphic representation of this model. The point here is not to propose individual courses, but instead to offer elements or threads that seem to be essential to a cohesive and coherent program of study. Four strands of professional preparation are important—(1) study in the arts and sciences and (2) study in the field of education, both common for all educators regardless of teaching discipline or grade level and subject- or level-specific pedagogy; (3) experience in a wide range of educational settings; and (4) time for focused reflection and

Figure 3.1. Model of Professional Teacher Preparation

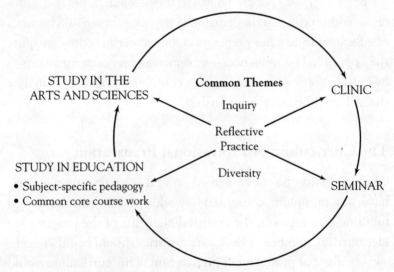

inquiry (seminar). Common themes in all—inquiry and reflection, equity and diversity—serve as adhesive to hold the four strands together, to give the professional preparation curriculum the coherence it requires. (Chapter Five provides details on how issues of equity and diversity have been incorporated into the teacher education program at the University of Connecticut.)

Educating Reflective, Inquiring Practitioners at the University of Connecticut

Organized around the themes of reflective practice, teacher inquiry, equity, and diversity, the University of Connecticut's teacher education program represents a complete redesign of the way classroom teachers have traditionally been prepared. Underlying much of the reform process at the university was a rejection of the traditional apprenticeship model on which most teacher education programs have been based; rather, we focused on the concept of teachers as professional educators, with special attention to the roles of reflection, curiosity, and altruism in promoting professional practice.[31] Our intention was to create a program that would provide students with a solid liberal arts base, extensive clinical experience in a variety of educational settings (including a mandatory urban placement for all students), and involvement in ongoing and increasingly sophisticated reflective practice throughout their preparation. The redesign of the teacher education program took place over three years and culminated in the fall of 1991 with the full implementation of an innovative, three-year integrated bachelor's/master's degree program. Students are admitted as juniors and depart after three years in the program with a bachelor's degree, a master's in education, and all the requirements for state certification.

Every phase of the teacher education program emphasizes analysis and reflection.[32] Throughout the program, all students keep journals, work in cohort groups with faculty members on problem analysis, prepare and discuss school-based case studies and narratives of critical incidents, design and conduct school-based inquiry projects, and engage in focused dialogue. The focus of the master's/internship year (the student's third year in the program) is to develop professional educators who will be capable of implementing models for teacher and school change, taking leadership roles, and conducting action research.

One of the major ways in which collaborative efforts have been undertaken and maintained in the University of Connecticut experience has been through the development of school-based research efforts. We have endeavored to increase the level of reflective practice of students, educators in the partnership schools, and faculty at the university through the use of different kinds of collaborative, school-based research projects.[33] We believe that combining the human, intellectual, and experiential resources of classroom teachers, school administrators, university faculty, and teachers-to-be offers a powerful base for the simultaneous renewal of schools and the university. Further, we believe that school-based research projects provide especially useful and compelling instances of the potential of truly collaborative school-university activities.[34] As Goodlad has compellingly argued:

> Schools must be centers or cultures of inquiry, renewing themselves continuously by addressing self-consciously the total array of circumstances constituting their business—and in this way become good. To be *very* good, schools must place education at the heart of renewal, vastly broadening their instructional practices and rejuvenating their curricula. This necessitates far more effective, comprehensive educator preparation programs than we now have. And these are possible only by closely linking schools and universities in the simultaneous process of renewal. . . . [35]

A key piece in our efforts to promote school-based research has been the core research course taught in the fifth year of the teacher education program. This course, team-taught by four faculty members with extensive experience conducting educational research, is designed to provide students with a broad overview of both traditional quantitative and qualitative/naturalistic research methodologies. Students learn the advantages and limitations of each type of research and design a study using the most appropriate methodology available to them. Supporting the research course is an intensive, small group seminar in which students receive extensive feedback related to both the design and conduct of their individual inquiry projects. In the seminar, students identify school-based research problems and formulate proposals for their inquiry projects. Readings in the seminar are designed to extend those in the core course and to help students relate research in teaching to the broader issues of equity and diversity. Students have read such works as *How We Think* (1910, revised 1933), by John Dewey; "Researching Change and Changing the Researcher" (1993), by Concha Delgado-Gaitan; "Fieldwork Enlightenment" (1995), by Barre Toelken; *Peripheral Visions* (1994), by Mary Catherine Bateson; *A Thrice-Told Tale: Feminism, Postmodernism, and Ethnographic Responsibility* (1992), by Margery Wolf; *Inside/Outside: Teacher Research and Knowledge* (1993), edited by Marilyn Cochran-Smith and Susan L. Lytle; and *Women's Ways of Knowing: The Development of Self, Voice, and Mind* (1986), by Mary Field Belenky, Blythe McVicker Clinchy, Nancy Rule Goldberger, and Jill Mattuck Tarule.[36]

Strand 1: Study in the Arts and Sciences

If teaching is at heart a moral and political matter, if teachers are moral and political agents, if the main purpose of schooling is to teach students their moral and intellectual responsibilities for living and working in a democracy, then what should be the liberal education of the intending teacher provided by the arts and sciences such that intending teachers can fulfill effectively and ethically their moral and political responsibilities as teachers?[37]

The role that the arts (including the fine arts) and sciences play in liberal education, and thus teacher education, cannot be overstated.[38] James O. Freedman describes the importance of a liberal education:

> A liberal education acquaints students with the cultural achievements of the past and prepares them for the exigencies of an unforeseeable future. It provides them with standards by which to measure human achievement. It fires their minds with new ideas—powerful and transcendent ideas that will trouble them, elevate them, and brace them for new endeavors. It offers students an opportunity to develop the humane empathy and moral courage required to endure uncertainty, disappointment, and suffering.[39]

Further, Freedman argues, a liberal education "helps students to develop an independent perspective for reflecting on the nature and texture of their lives. And it inspires students to delineate the foundations of the moral identity and to find their distinctive ways through the complicated and uncertain process by which intellectual and moral maturation occurs."[40] A teacher who is liberally educated, according to Freedman's definition, will be better able than one who is not to provide access to knowledge, thereby allowing future citizens to be "born." But making strong connections between the departments in the arts and sciences and schools of education has historically met with resistance and is most often "not part of a coordinated effort to prepare teachers for their role as stewards of renewing schools in a democracy."[41] Further, some of the reluctance to embed an understanding of subject matter in the education of educators emanates from those within the school of education itself. Yet teachers who lack a strong liberal arts background, as well as a firm grasp of what they are called on to teach, all too often find themselves trapped by the standard curriculum, with little of their own knowledge with which to expand and enrich the curriculum. On the other end of the scale are teachers like "Tom," who, according to Hugh Sockett, "demonstrate the depth of *knowledge and understanding* teachers have to have of what they teach. There is no substitute for this, and without it a teacher is something of a charlatan. Tom is so confident of his historical knowledge that he can translate it with such vigor (and justified license) to ensure that the subject is alive for his students."[42]

Strand 2: Course Work in the Field of Education

In our estimation, there are more commonalities to teaching across grade levels and disciplines than there are differences. Although this premise is certainly debated hotly and often, educators at the University of Connecticut begin with it when they design programs of study. We suggest a common core curriculum for all who would call themselves professional teachers.

A Common Core for All Educators

One important element is the study of learning and how it might be assessed or evaluated. This topic leads to discussions of both a theoretical and a practical nature. A common core curriculum would also include topics and assignments relative to the multicultural nature of today's schools and society and, consequently, how individual differences are accepted and accommodated. Within these discussions would be specific information about (but not limited to) students with special education needs and linguistic differences. The social context of schooling would be emphasized, along with issues of poverty, drugs, disease, and the like, because all of these affect children, families, communities, and, consequently, teachers and the schools they work in.

In this fast-paced world, a teacher education curriculum must include topics related to the role of technology. Teachers of the future must be able to access and teach the many new technologies available, and they must feel comfortable using the technologies. It is clear from our work and that of others that technology opens the world to many students who might otherwise be unable to gain access, such as those with physical or learning disabilities. It also has the potential to assist students with disabilities in expressing their ideas and knowledge. But educators must also understand the limitations and consequences of technology. They need to know when the teacher is a better conveyor of knowledge, when the teacher is a better motivator, and when the teacher has greater power to nurture.

As we have already suggested, the teacher should be quite capable of inquiring into his or her own teaching practice. Although learning to be a teacher-researcher cannot happen in one course, we believe that a structured classroom experience that provides a foundation for this practice is essential. Therefore, we suggest that a beginning course on teacher or action research serve as a springboard for other activities in this area. Similarly, becoming a teacher-leader—a teacher who can and will act as a steward of the schools—is certainly a part of the role of the teacher today and is a process that should begin in the core curriculum. Finally, and really the first item on the core agenda, there must be a firm foundation in the past and present philosophical underpinnings of the profession. These discussions lead to further deliberations regarding the ethics of teaching.

Subject-Specific Pedagogical Course Work

Having made the case that a common core of learning is essential to a coherent program of teacher education, we also recognize that within each of the teaching specialties is a body of knowledge and competence that is essential and must be included. We caution that these specific skills or competencies are often at the heart of the argument that we alluded to earlier. University faculty members and many elementary and secondary teachers, steeped in subject-specific traditions, may see their disciplinary identities as grounds for separating rather than merging programs preparing educators. There is a real danger in asking teachers, on the one hand, to integrate curriculum and to work collaboratively while, on another, insisting that they be content experts. Nel Noddings explains the dilemma:

> Teachers, like students, need a broad curriculum closely connected to the existential heart of life and to their own special interests. They should be able to provide an intelligent approach to the legitimate needs and questions of students.
>
> How should teachers be prepared for a program of this sort? Perhaps the most fundamental change required is to empower teachers as we want them to empower students. We do not need to cram their heads with specific information and rules. Instead we should help them learn how to inquire, to seek connections between their chosen subject and other subjects, to give up the notion of teaching their subject only for its own sake, and to inquire deeply into its place in human life broadly construed.[43]

Further, Noddings argues, this will mean "a different form of education. Teachers need an integrated form of education, not a highly specialized education concentrating on one discipline."[44] And so the debate comes full circle here. We have previously made the case for a solid foundation in the arts and sciences—for the educator to be broadly educated. Others, such as the Holmes Group, would agree.[45] Yet if we commit to the type of education described earlier by Noddings, Kerr, and others—one of caring or nurturing learning—then, as Noddings suggests, "We have to stop asking: 'How can we get kids to learn math?'" Rather, we should be asking, "How can my subject serve the needs of each of these students?"[46] And thus we will be forced, if we are to be both informed and caring, to come together with those in the arts and sciences to construct a curriculum that does both. A place such as the center of pedagogy put forth by Goodlad would surely be of great assistance.[47]

Strand 3: Clinical Experience

Providing future teachers with a planned sequence of clinical experiences prepares educators who are not solely second-grade teachers or high school social studies teachers. When we say "a planned sequence," we mean that these experiences for all educators, regardless of intended area of certification, should span the grades and disciplines, include experiences in urban settings, and entail work with students who have special education needs. These experiences should be directly tied to the course work and seminar that students find themselves in during any given semester. Most important, these experiences should be designed to move the future educator toward professional thinking and behavior relative to the moral dimensions of teaching. At the University of Connecticut, this means six semesters of increasingly challenging and focused clinical placements, including a full-year graduate internship following student teaching. A future elementary educator describes the importance of experience and, in particular, the internship year:

> Over the past academic year, I have had the challenging and exciting opportunity of working in an urban high school as a tutorial coordinator. This opportunity placed me in the role of a leader, alongside my partner. I felt [that] as a coordinator I gained leadership qualities that I hadn't achieved in my previous years. . . . True, I was a leader within my classroom, but I never worked with an entire staff or administration, which is what my present internship requires. . . . This is where I developed my leadership qualities. . . . I learned and internalized not only leadership, but organizational skills, stronger listening skills, rapport development skills, one-on-one interaction skills, and in a sense, business skills.[48]

Strand 4: Seminar

Goodlad has suggested that "a teacher education program cannot function effectively within the conventional regularities of classes and credits geared to sitting and listening." Rather, "a considerable part of the program is best carried out through seminars closely tied to field experiences," and reflection must be an integral part of the process.[49] We fully agree that the seminar strand of any professional preparation program is critical. A seminar, when tied directly to clinical experiences as well as course work, provides a forum for focused conversation and reflection and is a means to achieve levels of scholarship beyond the usual. In its best form it consists of serious students dedicated to a quest for the knowledge that represents their common interest. A seminar provides an opportunity for students and teachers to explore together the many facets of this common interest; ideally it is a collegium, with peers sharing authority and responsibility.

Dialogue and Conversation

Seminars can be designed to provide students with a forum for dialogue centering on current issues affecting the nature of our schools, the impact school designs have on the diverse populations in schools today, the moral and ethical issues facing educators in a democracy, and the ways in which teachers as leaders and researchers can be influential in changing how we view and conduct the practice of teaching. Ruth Grant, in a powerful analysis of "the ethics of talk," provides a clear definition of what is meant by "dialogue":

> Unlike debate, a dialogue is a conversation in which different opinions are critically evaluated, distinctions are made, and arguments and evidence are put forward with a view to reaching agreement on whatever comes to light as most reasonable—*and* with the expectation that something new and better will come to light. And unlike debate, dialogue requires the participants to conduct themselves ethically and autonomously in very important respects.[50]

She presses the importance of dialogue or conversation as it re-
lates to a "civics education": "Decent politics, and democratic politics particularly, is conducted through talk, and thus conversation
has an impact beyond the individual development of character.
Conversation is a civics education as well as a moral education because the capacity for conversation is a crucial public capacity."[51]

The "Dialogues on Transforming Education" between Ira Shor
and Paulo Freire in A *Pedagogy for Liberation* are one example that
we often use to demonstrate to students what we mean by conversation or dialogue. In this work, Freire tells Shor,

> In liberating education, we do not propose mere tech-
> niques for gaining literacy or expertise or professional
> skills or even critical thought. The methods of dialogi-
> cal education draw us into the intimacy of the society, a
> *raison d'être* of every object of study. Through critical di-
> alogue about a text or a moment of society, we try to re-
> veal it, unveil it, see its reasons for being like it is, the
> political and historical context of the material. This for
> me is an act of knowing, not a mere transfer-of-knowledge
> or a mere technique for learning the alphabet. The lib-
> erating course "illuminates" reality in the context of de-
> veloping serious intellectual work.[52]

One future educator discusses how dialogue with her teaching
partner assisted her in overcoming a feeling of isolation in times of
difficulty:

> Lately . . . I've been feeling disempowered and this an-
> noys me. I tried to come up with ways to rejuvenate my-
> self and regain some of the enthusiasm I've lost in the
> last several weeks. What I have found to be very benefi-
> cial is dialogue. My partner has been feeling the same
> way as I've been feeling. Talking to Lori and [her] em-

pathizing with me makes me realize that I am not alone. In teaching, one is *never* alone. Teachers form a community, we support and help each other along. When dialogue occurs, one begins to look for solutions to solve personal and professional problems. Together, Lori and I have been working to figure out ways to address the several issues that have been brought to our attention.[53]

Reading as Essential to Professional Behavior and Understanding

When reading is in the service of an interpreting community and not done in social or intellectual isolation, then reading becomes intelligent, for it becomes an active and articulate mediation between common sense and expertise. A community of peers—a pedagogic *polis*, if you will—supplies the necessary conditions for making reading social and intelligent. . . . Within a community, practical intelligence has an object and an occasion; without community, theoretic intelligence is stillborn.[54]

Reading is essential to all of the strands, but we have chosen to elaborate on it at this juncture because our collective experience tells us that the seminar is the place where reading can be used in a quite different way than it is in traditional course work. One of our master's interns told us: "This [internship] year has provided the most thought-provoking experiences in my life as an educator. In seminar we read interesting and applicable books and discussed their meaning as well as their relevance to our teaching practices. The books and the discussions about them expanded the scope of my vision and enabled me to examine events from many vantage points."[55]

We have suggested a number of readings in this chapter that have been useful in our own experience to stimulate conversation about the moral dimensions of teaching: equity and equal access to knowledge, ways of inquiring that go beyond the typical, our society and its cultural influence on the classroom, democracy in education, and the need to care for children as well as adults to nurture their learning. One future social studies/history teacher told us, "I found some of the books assigned to be truly enlightening (especially the poetry [by Langston Hughes]). Although I was aware of inequities based solely on race, socioeconomic status, and gender, I was not fully cognizant of their effect on schooling and society as a whole."[56]

Conclusion

In closing our discussion of the preparation of future educators who will be professional in their character and in their work, we must go back to the words of David Page. Teachers must be well educated and sufficiently experienced, but there must also be a "spirit" within the teachers to educate all in their care, to challenge the system when necessary, to inquire and reflect often on their craft, and to continue to learn for themselves. Environments committed to renewal are the places where future teachers should be encultured. Building centers for professional development that enhance the education of future educators and at the same time create nurturing environments for those who already call themselves professionals is the task to which we next turn.

4

Creating Educative Communities

Fostering a sense of community among individuals is essential to developing learning environments that support both adult and student learning. But as we are all too painfully aware, building communities of any sort is not without conflict. Which takes precedence, the will of all or individual freedom?[1] Will we remember, as Socrates reminds his friend Glaucon in Plato's *Republic*, that law has the power to influence men to bond together in common purpose through both persuasion and compulsion and, in so doing, share the benefits within the commonwealth?

> "My friend, you have again forgotten," I said, "that it's not the concern of law that any one class in the city fare exceptionally well, but it contrives to bring this about for the whole city, harmonizing the citizens by persuasion and compulsion, making them share with one another the benefit that each class is able to bring to the commonwealth. And it produces such men in the city not in order to let them turn whichever way each wants, but in order that it may use them in binding the city together."[2]

Centuries later, John Dewey addressed the same issue, linking the common good directly to schooling:

What the best and wisest parent wants for his own child, that must the community want for all of its children. Any other ideal for our schools is narrow and unlovely; acted upon, it destroys our democracy. All that society has accomplished for itself is put, through the agency of the school, at the disposal of its future members. . . . Here individualism and socialism are at one. Only by being true to the full growth of all individuals who make it up, can society by any chance be true to itself.[3]

If the teaching profession is to flourish, the community in which it lives and breathes must be educative—taking into account the needs of individuals within the context of the will of the larger community. This type of community would advantage individuals through the collection of knowledge and skills held by all its members. It would advance democracy through informed conversation by all citizens. This educational community would naturally have student learning at its core, but the concentric circles around this core would involve teachers, school administrators, university faculty, parents, community leaders, and citizens in continuous learning, through study, reflection, and inquiry. And these concentric circles of learning would be permeable: teachers would learn from parents, university faculty would learn from children, community leaders would learn from teachers, and the like. Unfortunately, our ways of thinking are not always that flexible. Yet we have begun to build these types of educative communities through partnerships of various sorts. Partnerships between business and schools have led educators to new ways of connecting educational goals with the needs of the business community. Collaborations between community agencies, such as hospitals or shelters for the homeless, and the schools have helped students to engage in the life of their community and connect these encounters to their learning in the classroom. Partnerships between schools and the colleges and universities that prepare future school personnel are also proving to be a means of connecting school renewal with the ongoing professional development of educators.

Linking Professional and School Renewal with Educative Communities

For professionals to learn about the standards and moral principles of their profession and act in compliance with those standards and principles, the environment must be supportive of their actions. Thus, the preparation of future professionals and the continuing development of those who already call themselves professional educators requires strong and deep connections among our nation's schools, institutions of higher learning, and their surrounding communities. In *The Ecology of School Renewal* (1987), *Educational Renewal: Better Teachers, Better Schools* (1994), and *In Praise of Education* (1997), John Goodlad makes the case for educative communities as healthy ecosystems—schools and communities that are caring, that nurture growth, and that are characterized by a moral connectedness that is manifested in a deep moral respect for self and others. He suggests that we need to create such environments in schools and communities as well as in the relationships between the two. He tells us that "to think systemically about educating is to think of a system of education that includes much more than schools. At the core of this system are educative communities of which schools are an important part."[4] But as Ernest Boyer suggests, "Community doesn't just happen, even in a small school. To be a true community, the institution must be organized around people, 'around relationships and ideas,' as Trinity University professor Thomas J. Sergiovanni puts it. Communities, he says, 'create social structures that bond people together in a oneness, and that bind them to a set of shared values and ideas.'"[5] Further, Daniel Perlstein, in a retrospective look at the New Deal–era educational experiment at Arthurdale, West Virginia, examines the importance of community and democracy within the confines of an environment that is inherently unequal:

> Community and democracy are both worthy educational ideals. Sometimes, they overlap. Community, however, marks borders and exclusion as well as inclusion. It is always therefore ambiguous, with the potential to foster citizen involvement, to facilitate demands for justice, or to mask social inequality. The efforts of school reformers are inevitably shaped by the political and social dynamics that contribute to the meaning of their work. Progressive education either challenges social divides, or it founders on them. Today, as in the 1930s, mass structural unemployment in American cities and economic insecurities throughout the country circumscribe the progressive impulse to create communities of learners. Now, as then, the improbable work of building broad communities against racism and class privilege is crucial to the moral and practical work of democratic educators.[6]

We have found that building professional learning communities that appear to have the potential to confront issues of inequality and racism can come about through students' studying and learning in cohort groups within partnership schools. This process of socialization into the teaching profession and the larger community of school is critical if, as Goodlad suggests, we are to allow teachers to "transcend their self-oriented student preoccupations to become more other-oriented in identifying with a culture of teaching."[7]

This *can* happen and *is* happening. Teacher education students are telling us about how working in a cohort group across disciplines in one urban partnership school—conducting research together and adding to the resources of the school—moves them to become more and more professional. One intern stated in a focus group interview that "the team and reflective practice were inseparable because we were always talking, reflecting on this and that." This finding is consistent with the move toward collaborative practices in schools and what Sandra Schecter and Shawn Parkhurst label "teacher-research groups," which make the important link between research, reflection, and groups working together: "Teacher-research groups are ideal vehicles for both reflecting ideologies of teaching . . . and for transforming these ideologies."[8] Over several years, a number of interns who worked at the same professional development school talked openly and consistently about the need for such a community of educators and the importance of working and learning in teams:

> School should feel like a community where people are tied together. I guess that's the beauty of a cohort. It makes you feel like you are part of something. It's not perfect. We've had arguments, but we've grown. You need to work with people to develop.[9]

> [Another] role that I find myself in is the role of a peer. The UConn [University of Connecticut] students have had some amazingly profound discussions. . . . I think these conversations are important as they supply us (or at least me) with a discourse that I may continue in my mind and in my journal as well as bring back to others if I want to. I've noticed that none of us is afraid to ask for or to offer help if it looks like it is needed. We are a constant source of support for each other away from the amniotic security of the university and I truly believe we derive strength from our numbers. Our conversations allow us to rethink and refocus in a way that would not be possible in isolation, and we flourish for it. It is the platform that makes all my other roles so strong and successful and I am thankful for it.[10]

As I reflect on the [internship] year and how I have
grown and what I have learned, many things come to
mind. First, I have realized how important it is to have a
strong cohort and group of colleagues to rely on for help,
advice, and encouragement. We were always supportive
of one another. We learned together and developed
strong friendships. By helping one another we were able
to grow as teachers, professionals, students, and individuals. . . . I never realized how important cohorts are until
this year.[11]

Finally, two interns commented on the power of cohorts in the
development of intellectual communities and, most important, the
ability of these teams to provide all children with a more equitable
education:

From my peers I have learned a great deal. The community that we are allowed to thrive in has given me a re-
newed inspiration for the future of the profession I have
chosen. I cannot remember having worked with such a
fired and determined group of people. The care and love
that each of my peers has displayed this semester in regard to students as well as toward each other has opened
a new door to me. The strong ties that I have witnessed
allow me a glimpse of what I can expect to share with
others in the future. I feel that we have developed an intellectual community that could move mountains.[12]

Together the team supported each other, filling in for
each other, advising each other, all in the effort of improving the educational situation for as many students
as we humanly could. The students were the priority and
the focus of all of our efforts. It was a great source of
pride for me to have been part of a team that was so ded-

icated, in a highly moral sense, to the educational welfare of dozens of children.[13]

Yes, educators are making progress on the agenda of forming educational communities with a moral mission, yet they still have
many miles to go. It is our sincere hope that building educative
communities—places where professionals can learn and practice
their craft at the same time—will become the cornerstone for the
simultaneous renewal of schools and the university community that
prepare future teachers. But for the transformation of professional
environments to take place, professionals working in schools must
first be fully aware of the social context in which the school re-
sides.[14] Just as the broader educational community should have an
in-depth understanding of our nation's attempts to uphold democratic principles, with all the inherent problems that poses, so should
groups of local educators understand the difficulties that communities encounter in providing equitable educational opportunities for
all the citizens of a particular community, school, or classroom. "The
dynamic, renewing school," John Goodlad explains, "is one self-
consciously connected to society's expectations for it and to autho-
rized convictions regarding sound educational practices."[15]

The Social Context of Schooling

I . . . have to be more or less critical concerning how our
society is working. I need critical understanding of the
very ways the society works, in order for me to understand how the education I am involved in works in the
global context and in the context of the classroom. In
the last analysis, we change ourselves to the extent we
become engaged in the process of social change. . . . To
separate the global dynamics of social change from our
educational practice is a mistake.[16]

Advancing the notion of educative communities as the social context within which teaching and learning takes place is essential. Clearly, the social context of schooling, dictated by an unequal distribution of resources and standardized curricula, fosters a multitude of unequal educational opportunities.[17] Changing the current situation will require the coordinated effort of many people, but teachers can and should play a central role. Teachers who have a clear understanding of the social context or ecology of their own classrooms as well as the surrounding community will be better able to make professional decisions that are culturally sound.[18] Thus, the classroom teacher must be sensitive, knowledgeable, and in tune with the many individual cultures found within the classroom. Further, the larger social context of the school, the community, and those institutions of higher education preparing future teachers needs to become coordinated in creating more equitable school environments.[19]

We agree with Paulo Freire that separating "global dynamics of social change from our educational practice is a mistake" in designing programs of professional preparation.[20] Therefore, we must infuse the idea of schooling in a social context into the curriculum of future teachers and professional development opportunities for teachers.

Inquiry and reflection are essential pieces of professional practice. If we agree with Goodlad that educators have a moral obligation to provide "access to knowledge" for all students,[21] then educators must challenge the current educational culture that continues to segregate and isolate students from access to equal educational opportunities. For teachers to play a key role in changing these greater societal problems, they must act not only as "good" teachers, but also as responsible citizens, being stewards of their classrooms and school communities as well as being reflective and curious about the social contexts and cultural norms of their teaching environment. C. A. Bowers and David J. Flinders connect the ability to be reflective about these matters to the capacity for making professional decisions that are culturally sound:

> The importance of taking into account the context of the classroom as an essential aspect of professional decision making is one of the main reasons we have been critical of classroom management techniques and teaching strategies that are often represented in teacher education textbooks as having universal applicability. As we have attempted to show, each classroom ecology involves patterns of thought and communication . . . that are influenced by the primary culture of both students and the teacher as well as other cultural factors relating to age, gender, social class, and so forth. Personal idiosyncrasies relating to mood, style of humor, and ways of thinking and responding to the myriad events that characterize interpersonal life in school and the larger society are also part of classroom ecology.[22]

Two master's interns preparing to be elementary and special educators, respectively, address these issues in their reflective journals, writing about student diversity and the social context of the school. Both spent their internships in an inner-city high school. They speak quite powerfully about the impact that poverty, gangs, violence, and other social problems can have on the denial of freedom as well as their own preconceived notions about students:

> I am working [in a tutoring program] with students, the majority of whom are living lives I couldn't possibly imagine. . . . I have met a gang member and admit to my intimidation. I heard he has a bad temper, but I have put my biases aside and have discovered a very nice gentleman. He is quiet but friendly, and I love making him

> laugh. He is one of our drop-in students; he likes to come and talk. I haven't seen as much gang activity as I expected within the high school. It is a very ordinary school in my opinion. . . . The students are all amazing to me and have so much potential. Each one is unique and has taught me something.[23]

> No matter how much certain segments of society alienate these children, their goals and their dreams are no different than anyone else's. . . . Many of these students resented the existence of gangs and death in their neighborhoods because . . . these things took away certain freedoms that all children should have the opportunity to enjoy—such as playing in their neighborhoods or simply walking down the street without having to fear the possibility that death could be around the corner.[24]

Although we believe quite strongly that experience is critical to a future teacher's understanding of the social context of the classroom and the community, we have found that seminar conversations (as discussed in Chapter Three) stimulated by thought-provoking readings push students to think more broadly and deeply about these matters. Among the readings that have been helpful are *Billy* (1993), by Albert French; *Local Knowledge* (1983), by Clifford Geertz; *Schooling Homeless Children* (1994), by Sharon Quint; *There Are No Children Here* (1991), by Alex Kotlowitz; *Savage Inequalities* (1991) and *Amazing Grace* (1996), by Jonathan Kozol; and *The Education of Little Tree* (1976), by Forest Carter. Discussions in one such university seminar, in conjunction with a year-long clinical experience in a city high school, prompted an intern preparing to be a special educator to tell us of his learning about urban youths, the culture of the school, and the need to question one's teaching practice constantly:

Through my interactions with students, I have developed a greater understanding of what an urban high school is all about and urban life, in general, is like. I have learned that all youths are much smarter than we give them credit for. I have developed a better understanding of the importance of interdependence among all. We are all very dependent on each other—teachers and students alike. The opportunities [provided in this high school] gave me the insight to question my own actions and to evaluate my performance and decisions. . . . Through all of these interactions I learned about the culture and customs of this school and the system. Some of these lessons were hard to swallow and others were just waiting to be realized. But each of them could have been learned only by being where I was, in every sense of the phrase.[25]

Learning to be a teacher should include guided study in how to be a teacher-researcher. In our experience, inquiry projects conducted by master's interns have reflected the commitment to a better understanding of the social context within which schooling transpires. Students have studied different cultures, examined the impact of gangs on the schools, and looked at intervention programs and their effects on families. They have been troubled by elementary and high school students who fear for their lives and have wondered about how these fears influence the students' lifelong goals. These studies have looked outside the classroom—and sometimes the school itself—and then made connections back to the stewardship that educators must practice. A selection of student inquiry projects focusing on the social context of schooling helps to illustrate the types of action research that can be undertaken:

- "The Effects of Students' Perceptions of Their Life Span on Their Future Goals"

- "Fear, Threats, Gangs (Violent Social Groups), and Urban Schools: Comparative Characteristics and Interventions in the Northeast Corridor (US) and Southern England"

- "Effects of a Home Visit Program on 'At-Risk' Students and Their Families"

- "Journey to Moscow and Back"

- "The Cycle of Violence"

Fostering Professional Development Through School-University Partnerships

In recent years, school-university partnerships have been seen as a viable force behind change in the education profession in both P–12 schools and in institutions of higher education (IHEs). They have also been viewed as essential to fostering educative communities that are more equitable and responsive to the needs of the children throughout the nation. Over the past decade, national organizations and state departments of education have advocated and in some cases mandated such collaborations. Groups such as the National Network for Educational Renewal, the Holmes Partnership, the American Association of Colleges for Teacher Education, the National Commission on Teaching & America's Future, and others have provided models that schools and institutions of higher education can use to build and sustain such partnerships in professional development schools (PDSs). They have also helped to show why change in the profession will have greater power if educators at all levels work with one another. Yet, as Roy J. Creek reminds us,

> The problems facing American education did not happen overnight. . . . Consequently, lasting reform will probably have to be systematic and incremental. Because

it was conceived to be an entity whose priorities are longevity and inquiry, the properly constituted PDS could become a key to educational reform if specific attitudinal and policy changes are made. The attitudinal changes are most needed in the university community where needs for funding and recognition serve to subvert initiatives for legitimate reform. The policy changes are needed in teacher unions and administrative structures that restrict the activities and imaginations of classroom teachers.[26]

Crossing the cultural barriers between schools and universities is not easily accomplished, but partnerships (collaborations for educational change) have the potential to effect systemic change.[27] Those who have worked in this fledgling arena of professional development are fully aware that partnerships are neither easy to build nor easy to sustain.[28] Establishing trusting relationships,[29] recognizing cultural differences,[30] building social capital,[31] and breaking perceived roles between professionals in the schools and university faculty become indispensable if partnerships are to be anything more than traditional in nature. Goodlad states: "In paying more attention to building social capital through the cultivation of educative communities, we may be less inclined to blame the schools for our malaise and to hold them responsible for the nation's well-being. We can then reasonably expect of them fulfillment of their unique educational mission. Healthy nations have healthy schools. Healthy schools and robust democracies go hand in hand."[32]

Centers for Professional Development

Professional development centers provide the real-life context for preparing teachers and initiating the simultaneous renewal of schools and the teaching profession. These school-university partnerships must be nurtured for extended periods of time and must actively work to break cultural barriers by establishing trusting relationships and building social capital. Partners strive to engage one another in conversation about such things as the moral dimensions of teaching and the simultaneous renewal of schools and the teaching profession. These centers for professional development would ideally be more than partnerships between one university and one school; they would be centers where educational community could be built. They would then be quite powerful in assisting professional educators to acquire a broader understanding of the wider community of learning necessary for school renewal. Marleen Pugach and Barbara Seidl summarize the influence that these relationships can have on future teachers' understanding of the social contexts in which children are educated: "Partnership schools can serve as holistic situations that provide prospective teachers with opportunities to become 'students of a sociocultural context' in which they can explore issues of social and cultural diversity."[33] We believe that experiences in these settings are key to future school professionals' gaining insight into the social context of schooling.

Although partnerships have the potential to alter the educational circumstances of children, youths, and adults dramatically, Hugh Sockett cautions that educators face many challenges in building partnerships both across and within communities. Among those challenges is the independent commitment to this work: "Partnerships attempt to forge a unified community recognizable by common values, ideals and commitments already shared by many individuals professionally committed to education and teaching. Yet too often the work of creating partnerships is left to independent individuals with the result that new institutional models of collegiality and mutual responsibility are not developed or installed."[34]

It is important at this point to back up for a moment and summarize the various models or instances of university-school partnerships that have been proposed and that exist. Many partnerships call themselves "professional development schools," but what does this really mean?[35] In *Tomorrow's Schools: Principles for the Design of Professional Development Schools*, members of the Holmes Group present their view of these professional arrangements in the following way: "By 'Professional Development School' we do not mean just a laboratory school for university research, nor a demonstration school. Nor do we mean just a clinical setting for preparing student and intern teachers. Rather, we mean all of these together: a school for the development of novice professionals, for continuing development of experienced professionals, and *for the research and development of the teaching profession*."[36] Further, the Holmes Group looks "at the Professional Development School as a model of learning community that will act as a bridge in the long process of creating a democratic culture."[37]

In an effort to assist school-university partnerships in evaluating partner schools, Richard W. Clark identified four purposes of school-university partnerships:

1. Preparing teachers (and other educators, including principals, counselors, librarians, and a variety of student-service specialists)
2. Providing continuing education for professionals
3. Conducting inquiry
4. Providing an exemplary education for all P–12 students enrolled[38]

A more detailed compilation of characteristics of professional development schools is under development and evaluation by the National Council for Accreditation of Teacher Education (NCATE). In its 1997 "Draft Standards for Identifying and Supporting Quality Professional Development Schools," the council identifies three stages of development: "pre-threshold, threshold, and quality attainment."[39] In summary, at the pre-threshold stage of development, "individuals build relationships, mutual values and understandings, and early collaboration between school and university teachers takes shape."[40] At the threshold stage, NCATE suggests that the following conditions be in place:

1. An agreement which commits school, school district, union/professional organization, and the university to the basic mission of a PDS
2. A commitment by the partners to the critical attributes of a PDS
3. A positive working relationship and a basis for trust between partners
4. The achievement of quality standards by partner institutions as evidenced by regional, state, national, or other review
5. An institutional commitment of resources to the PDS from school and university[41]

Finally, "standards for quality review" of the essential attributes of a PDS are written in the following areas:

- Learning community

- Collaboration

- Accountability and quality assurance

- Organization, roles, and structure

- Equity[42]

There are increasing examples of university-school collaboration that are designed to incorporate the purposes of such partnerships as delineated by Clark and NCATE. For example, Robert Patterson, dean of the David O. McKay School of Education at Brigham Young University (BYU), has described the impact of the BYU–Public School Partnership. One of the points that he stresses is that inquiry can be an "instrument of change": "Teachers have been helped to see how their questions relating to their own practice and student learning are vital to the improvement of children's learning. By expressing their questions about what they are doing, teachers and professors are opening themselves to a sharing and re-fining of professional knowledge which then becomes a basis for their own continuing lifelong learning."[43]

As another example, the Hartford–University of Connecti-cut Professional Development Center has put forth the following mission:

The Hartford Professional Development Center is a col-laboration among school professionals and university fac-ulty and students designed to enhance public education. We are collectively committed to achieving excellence and equity in education for *all students*. It is the intent of the Professional Development Center to move beyond a traditional university-school relationship toward the cre-ation of a partnership dedicated to change within schools and in teacher preparation.

The Professional Development Center (PDC) allows for supervised clinical experiences in the preparation of prospective teachers and other educational profession-als. The PDC is an environment in which research-based instructional practices and programs can be observed and experienced by those preparing for professional careers in education. University and school personnel work to-gether to identify educational dilemmas and propose meaningful solutions, thereby creating a school commu-nity in which success is commonplace and failure to learn is significantly reduced. Dialogue on all levels, re-search on current educational practice, and continual questioning and reflection form the basis for the PDC.

Within this partnership we share a common vision in the revitalization of urban school environments and in the preparation of professionals who will be leaders in these schools. Specifically, we are attempting:

1. To provide the best possible environment for student academic learning and personal self-fulfillment;
2. To provide opportunities for preservice preparation and career-long professional development; and
3. To conduct collaborative research and development activities which will advance theory and practice in urban education.[44]

In summary, we posit a number of features essential to creating partnerships, changing the cultures of both the school and the university, and thereby beginning to create educative communities:

- Deep reflection about teaching and learning are key.

- Collaborative inquiry is essential.

- Colleagues must respect and be civil to one another. They must learn to work together.

- Individual difference must be both understood and respected.

- Conversation about teaching and learning must be fostered.

- Educators have a moral obligation to each child, to his or her family, and to the community in which the school is located.

- Most critical, democratic ideals and principles must be practiced.

Advancing Professionalism Through School-University Partnerships

John Goodlad observes that "the critical question is whether the collaborating institutions will see sufficient gain in the marriage to motivate the sharing of currently exclusive areas of turf, the candid confrontation of long-established practices that must be changed, and the necessary commitment of resources."[45] From among the answers that could be given to the question Goodlad poses, we have chosen to discuss how three aspects of professionalism can be strengthened through school-university partnerships, thereby providing a rationale for working in such structures to advance the profession. First, educators must move toward a habit of inquiry and reflection that is collaborative and valuable to the children and youths of our nation (see Chapter Three). Second, they must value equity, diversity, and instruction that promotes access to knowledge for all (see Chapter Five). Third, they will need to reorganize time and demeanor (see Chapter Six). Each of these is necessary if we are to change the character of the education profession.

Creating Centers for Inquiry

As educators in schools and IHEs move toward a habit of inquiry and reflection that is collaborative and valuable to the children and youths of our nation, they must consider how they work with one another. In creating a collaborative culture of educational inquiry, professional teachers are asked not only to be teachers but also to be researchers about their teaching.[46] At the same time, university faculty have traditionally been the ones who have conducted research about education, about how children learn, and about how children might best be instructed. The world of educational research is fraught with myths about research design, the power of a particular statistical procedure, and the need for control. Yet for most teachers, these issues are of little importance if the research does not inform their professional practice. The good news here is that much of this is changing. Teachers are conducting action-based inquiry into the organization of their schools and the instructional effectiveness of their classrooms. Examples can be found in professional journals, in books about teachers and their work, and at local, state, and national conferences.

Unfortunately, many faculty members at the university have only begun to change the way they conduct and view educational research. It is not clear whether university researchers view their work as participatory, even though there are numerous examples from sociology and anthropology. "Tragically," writes Sockett,

> the university study of education, as of many other subjects, is dominated by its own version of political correctness. I refer not to long-haired, left-wing sociologists to whom this weakness is usually attributed, but to adherents of positivist epistemology. It is almost a "political tyranny" that obliges faculty to publish in the "right" journals and to avoid work with practitioners or on teacher research if they want to get tenure. That weakness is manifest in the hierarchical attitudes the epistemology engenders. Not only do academics fail to be deeply and collegially involved in uses of practice, but they also seem to find the writings of teachers only worth reading if the teachers are their students. Both these characteristics are part of an epistemological dominance.[47]

Yet, as with the changes that are occurring in the area of teacher research and inquiry, teacher educators in the university are making progress—some as a direct consequence of professional connections made through school-university partnerships. Although qualitative methodologies and action-based research are not always regarded as "real" research, they are taking on a new mantle within academe. Much discussion about collaborative, action-based, and qualitative research has taken place in professional journals such as *Educational Researcher*.[48] It is time for these discussions to be taken seriously, for if educators are to do research about important educational issues, they must first consider what these issues actually are. Researchers in higher education might be wise to ask a teacher or two what they think is important to their teaching and to the children in their classroom. And, of course, if they do this work through partnerships, then the power of the research will be multiplied. As Goodlad so convincingly argues:

> The central thesis is that schools must be centers or cultures of inquiry, renewing themselves continuously by addressing self-consciously the total array of circumstances constituting their business—and in this way become good. To be *very* good, schools must place education at the heart of renewal, vastly broadening their instructional practices and rejuvenating their curricula. This necessitates far more effective, comprehensive educator preparation programs than we now have. And these are possible only by closely linking schools and universities in the simultaneous process of renewal. . . . [49]

It stands to reason that if teacher educators prepare teachers to be inquiring professionals and if faculty in higher education connect with like-minded school colleagues, then possibly they will have collective force in creating habits of inquiry in educators. Rick Abrams, who prepared to be both an elementary and secondary English educator as well as a special education teacher, discussed the value of conducting a piece of research within a partnership school as a part of his professional preparation:

> The manner in which my research project developed would never have come about without the permission to experiment and discover for myself what my interests were. I was to experience first-hand the beauty of "discovery learning." . . . It was nice to be permitted the keys to my own success. Is there a greater feeling than that which comes from the knowledge that you have the ability to design, implement and carry to the end your own research project? This must be what they mean by "empowerment."[50]

Fostering Equitable Educational Environments

Creating educational environments that are equitable, celebrate diversity, and ensure all children equal access to knowledge is a goal that is embedded in our democracy. Yet we know from our history and from present inequities in our nation's schools that not all children have equal access to knowledge, school resources vary dramatically, and not everyone in this great nation celebrates diversity. There are still those who believe that girls cannot learn mathematics as well as boys can, and there are some who would continue to place students with disabilities in segregated environments. We should all reflect on our nation's past errors in this regard—for example, the circumstances that led to *Brown* v. *Board of Education*—and look to the future. But to look to the future, members of the teaching profession must have the knowledge and compassion to advance equitable educational opportunities for all.

In this regard, the knowledge that teachers have about their work, democracy, educating future citizens to enter the human conversation, the arts and sciences, and the pedagogy of teaching are all parts of what might be deemed professional knowledge. Of equal weight here are the educators' and the educational communities' attitudes toward diversity. Equal access to knowledge cannot be realized if those imparting and constructing this knowledge do not believe that all people have the right to that knowledge. Experience is a critical factor in changing attitudes that are inherently discriminatory. Therefore, work in school-university partnerships that represent diverse populations and educational dilemmas is one way to ensure that future teachers have the opportunity to modify attitudes that might be less than accommodating. One University of Connecticut student who was preparing to be an elementary educator chose to spend his internship year working with inner-city middle school students with special education needs "because," he wrote, "I wanted to get a background in technology, but also because I wanted to learn more about special education and get a flavor and sensitivity for the role of a special educator."[51] While running a computer lab for these students, he conducted an inquiry project dealing with how teachers, technology, and individual student attention influence children to remain in or to leave school. He commented,

> My research was a highlight of my experience at Quirk. I thoroughly enjoyed my interviews and observations with the students I was able to serve. It was exciting to watch my research questions and interview questions come to life through the words and actions of my students. They have helped me realize the benefits and downfalls of computers as well as the necessity for tolerance in our society and schools. I think the most important thing I have learned this year is how exciting diversity in education is and can be. As I close this paper, I leave you with this. These are the words that I live by, but they have become especially meaningful since my being in Hartford and at the University of Connecticut: "Voici mon secret. Il est très simple: on ne voit bien qu'avec le coeur. L'essentiel est invisible pour les yeux." [Here is my secret. It is very simple: one can see only with the heart. What is important is invisible to the eyes.] From Saint-Exupéry, *Le Petit Prince*.[52]

Another intern who chose to spend her internship year in a city environment reflected on how this experience allowed her to understand that city schools are often misunderstood and, further, that student concerns have commonalities around the world:

> Entering Bulkeley High School [in Hartford, Connecticut], I had many prior assumptions about an inner-city environment. Having grown up in a suburban area, I was nervous and did not know what to expect. I saw Bulkeley

High School as a scary place and was uncertain if I was going to be able to relate with the students. . . . Throughout the year, I came to realize that Bulkeley was a safe environment and that learning was occurring as it would in any high school. I was able to relate well with all of my students, and they grew to respect and trust me. [In] my free time, I often was found talking with students and getting to know them better. I wanted to find out everything that I could and learn about growing up in an urban environment. Quickly, I found out that the majority of their concerns were the same as mine while in high school. . . . My experience at Bulkeley gave me the opportunity to connect with all types of students. I learned things that one cannot learn in the classroom, things that must be experienced.[53]

Reorganizing Professional Time and Demeanor

The reorganization of professional time and demeanor is essential if educators are to move beyond old paradigms of professionalism. Punching the time clock should not be part of the behavior of a professional. The paucity of time for school professionals to work with one another is often cited as a major reason that change in professional behavior cannot take place. It is very apparent that in many schools this is the case. Teachers have the awesome responsibility of educating and caring for large numbers of children every day and are now being asked to take on additional roles and responsibilities within the school. One teacher implores the "system" to provide more time to reflect on education and teaching "so teachers could, for a brief precious moment, talk to each other about why they do what they do. . . . We don't do that—we don't have time."[54]

For teachers to have more time to work with and learn from one another, and thereby renew the profession, methods of conducting in-service education will require serious revamping and expansion. Much of a teacher's life is spent in relative isolation, with little time for dialogue and reflection. In this chapter, we have lamented the lack of community and the paucity of conversation among educators. But there are educators who refuse to accept such solitary environments. One of these, a future mathematics educator, explains,

> Sharing knowledge in the field of education should be our greatest weapon against poor teaching or stagnant practices. However, it is the most underutilized tool in many of the schools that I have taught or observed in. . . . This [sharing] is the way I want to give of myself in the future because I do not feel that teaching should be competition between teachers but rather a collaboration of creative minds that are striving to educate to a level of excellence. I plan to place myself within a group of teachers who feel the same way and try to encourage other teachers to join in a healthy community for teachers and students.[55]

Clearly the nature of a teacher's professional character and demeanor is in flux—partly because of new teachers who see an alternative to the traditional isolation of teaching.

Professionals in higher education have a similar history of autonomy in their research and teaching. Not often enough have faculty members from IHEs engaged themselves in sustained ways in the work of schools. Yet those whose life's work is education must question why time spent in schools and research conducted about schools are not valued. Why could not university faculty fulfill their responsibilities to teaching, service, and research by working in collaboration with a school or set of schools? Why do university faculty consider work in schools to be more work? It might, in fact, be less—just a different way of thinking about the character of that work. We suggest that time is at such a scarcity for teachers and university faculty partly because of their own perceptions and attitudes. Before educators say that they do not have the time or that their work will not be valued, they must look hard and long at themselves and ask, "Is our behavior professional?" or "Are we just too comfortable in our old ways?" Work in university-school partnerships may assist them in answering these questions. As one teacher in an urban partnership responded when asked to speak about the role of inquiry in the teaching profession: "It [inquiry] is very important because it maintains a dynamism of trying to find new ways and better ways of teaching and communicating. And I think it is more than passing on information, but finding ways of teaching people to be self-sufficient. . . . So we don't control their lives but show them that they can do it on their own. I see research and teaching going together as participatory research." Speaking about the connection of the partnership to this idea, the teacher remarked,

> I think it is a positive one. I know that there are other people who don't think the same way. Usually those are the people in the retirement club. . . . If they had been in the frame of mind of participatory research from the beginning—like the new people that are coming out with this strength—they wouldn't be old in the sense of thinking, of their approach to students. They become old and obsolete because they stop researching. They stop looking for a new way. . . . It's not really the age, it's the mentality. . . . One of the greatest things of this partnership is that it keeps us on our toes.[56]

A Story of Community, Partnership, and Professionalism

We would be quite naive to think that partnerships are panaceas—that forming partnerships will lead to change for the better or that they alone will advance the notion of educative communities. Nevertheless, many of us have witnessed the significant changes, both small and large, that can transpire as a result of the collaboration among professionals in these two intersecting worlds of education.

Following is a description of one such partnership: the story of
Athena, a teacher education student, and the school, community,
and classroom she worked in. She describes one incident during her
graduate internship that exemplifies how a partnership can contribute to the preparation of a new professional educator and to the
professional community. This story also shows how partnerships advance the professional development of the university faculty and
teachers working in them, how they enhance the professional character of the school, how they can involve parents and community,
and, most important, how partnerships affect individual students in
the classroom. Creating environments that are both collaborative
and professional will require the strength and voices of many. As
Hugh Sockett has observed, they cannot be sustained by one or two
individuals.[57]

Athena was enrolled in the five-year teacher preparation program at
the University of Connecticut, preparing to be an English educator.
She did her student teaching at Bulkeley High School in Hartford,
Connecticut. Following this experience, she chose to work in a special education cluster during her internship year in the same school.

Bulkeley High School is permeated by the beauty of diversity, and
the teachers, administrators, and students have been intimately involved in creating a nurturing educational environment. Driving up to
Bulkeley, one sees a fortress: a large semimodern building with few
windows, with painted-over graffiti, filling an entire city block. It is an
ominous sight to the newcomer. The school is surrounded by a community plagued by poverty and the violence of gangs and drugs. One
parks behind the school and walks up three flights (from the base-
ment to the second floor) in a wide but dark stairwell. Then the door
opens onto a large, well-lighted entryway to the main office. Plants
and trophies fill this space. Discussion and laughter—among teachers and students and among those from Bulkeley and those from the
university—can be heard. One has moved past the outward trap-
pings of Bulkeley High School into the "Bulkeley family."

Bulkeley is one of three high schools in Hartford. Of Connecticut's six major cities, Hartford ranks highest in the percentage of single-parent families, births to teens, the number of unemployed young adults, crime, and school dropouts. Hartford is the fourth-poorest city of its size in the United States, with 28 percent of the population living below the poverty level. The eighteen hundred students at Bulkeley speak many languages; most speak Spanish, and for a large portion, English is a second language. A majority of the students have moved several times, many work, and many have children of their own. Almost 40 percent of the student body receives some form of special, remedial, or bilingual education. Test scores are below the national average, and a high percentage of those who enter as ninth graders never graduate.

But the family at Bulkeley is more than statistics. It is one of great diversity, in both language and culture. It is one striving to be better. It is one that hosts students and their teachers from Russia, Puerto Rico, Poland, and Italy. Its own students have traveled, with the help of dedicated teachers and the partnership with the university, to places far from the Hartford city limits. The school principal often says that the students and teachers of the Bulkeley family have been given the important responsibility of preparing a future generation of teachers. And thus, the daunting problems of Bulkeley are obstacles to overcome together. They are problems that must be countered with deep pockets of hope; most important, they must not become reasons for withdrawal—for not having time.

The university's partnership with Bulkeley has been in existence since 1988. When it began, we were determined to make this partnership a successful one and committed ourselves for the long term.

At Bulkeley High School, Athena chose to work with two special education teachers who had collaborated with university faculty in the design of a new cluster program for entering ninth graders in at-risk situations. All have severe behavioral and learning disabilities. Many of these young people speak limited English, others have difficulty reading and writing, and the majority have been in trouble both inside and outside school. Yet two dedicated teachers felt that more could be done for these students. And thus Athena, a future English teacher, and Christen, a fellow intern from the university preparing to be a special educator, opted to work in this new program. They created integrated instructional units, helped set the rules of classroom behavior, conducted research about the program's first year, and in so doing became professional educators. Athena's and Christen's involvement in this high school and in this classroom exemplify how partnerships can change the culture of professionalism.

Athena's story addresses many of the issues we have already discussed in this book: teacher time, professional demeanor, equitable access to knowledge, and habits of inquiry and reflective thinking. It describes how Athena and her colleagues have advanced an educative community, where student diversity is valued and where knowledge is available to all.

Athena's Story

Well here I am, once again, analyzing my accomplishments to date. Since the beginning of the semester, many people—friends and strangers alike—have asked me what I'm doing. And I have noticed that after I begin to explain the program that Christen and I have developed along with two Bulkeley teachers and faculty from the university, people have strange expressions on their faces. I could never really tell what the expressions were saying until they asked me where I was teaching. Then I recognized the expression as confusion. There is something about teaching "at-risk" students in an inner city that brings puzzlement to the minds of many:

"Why would an intelligent young woman with a good head on her shoulders want to work in a seemingly frustrating position, constantly banging her head against a wall?"

"No one can help those kids, they have failed for a reason, and they will continue to fail."

"Your heart is in the right place, but you will burn out soon. You can't save the world."

These are just a sample of the questions and unsolicited thoughts I receive constantly. I feel as though I am always justifying what I have chosen to do for my lifetime—to teach. I want to teach where I am needed and where I feel I can give the most to my students.

Christen and I have worked hard to make our program a success. If we feel some aspect of it is not working well, we adjust it on the spot and try again. We have never given up on a student or on our ability to reach a student. We do have terrible days when we question our abilities and our students' desire to learn. But, we have never said that they cannot learn. . . . If we have not accomplished anything else, we have been able to convey to them that we have faith in them as learners and as individuals.

If you walk into our often-noisy classroom and see Christen and me hopping from desk to desk engaging and reengaging students; if you see us take a student aside to give him or her a breather or pep talk; if you see us in a ransacked classroom, slouched in chairs, looking as if we just ran a marathon, then we have done something right that day. It is true that our classroom operates differently from the average one, but that is because our students operate differently from the average student: not on a lesser or negative scale, just an alternative one. As an example, I will give a description of our banquet.

We celebrated the conclusion of our multicultural unit with a world feast. It was an unexpected success. After reminding the students for two weeks of our upcoming banquet and their need to inform and invite their parents, their less-than-appreciative interest worried me. We had invited quite a few administrators and guests, and as of the day before the banquet, we only had two definite dishes, besides our own, and no parents coming. I was debating whether or not we should cancel and save our students the embarrassment. But I decided that I would give them one more chance and gave them the best "This is for all your hard work, this is for you," speech I could muster. But I think one of the students' words of wisdom did the trick: "Yo, if we don't bring any food, we will only look stupid to the people that are coming." If these kids are lacking in any area, it is definitely not in self-pride.

The next day I was extremely nervous. I went to the Home Economics room and started to warm up the four dishes that had been brought. Eventually, as the morning progressed, dish after dish began to come in, each accompanied by a sheepish grin from one of the students. In total, 17 of the 19 dishes came in, and we had one of our best days of attendance. I was so pleased with the students as I stirred yellow rice and tested the warmth of West Indian curried chicken. Then, when I brought all the food upstairs to commence the feasting, I was hit with another unbelievable sight: half of the students' parents were there to eat lunch with us. The room was full of people and aromatic dishes. Many people came up to us and congratulated us on our success, but I told them it was the students who deserved the praise and made that announcement while everyone was enjoying their lunch.

It was not until after the banquet was over that I discovered how proud of the students I was. Mrs. Camargo and Mrs. Bulkeley (the two special educators who teach in this class) filled me in on little stories of how some meals arrived. José, one of our more leaderlike, "I haven't got time for anyone or anything," types, asked his mother to make flan. She made two plates of it, and José, who absolutely refuses to be seen walking to school (uncool), decided he couldn't be late, so he walked to school carrying both plates of flan.

Tony, who was absent the day of my final plea for food, came to school without a dish. When he realized what was going on, he ran down to the office, called his mom, and pleaded with her to quickly make something and come to school. Tony impatiently waited in front of the school until his mother arrived.

And Paul, whose mother could not make anything because she worked very long hours, felt as though he did not deserve to eat anything, since he did not contribute to the feast. He believed that if he did not work to contribute as the others did, then he did not have the right to take the rewards of that work. Now, I challenge anyone who thinks that these kids have no respect for anyone and think of no one except themselves; Paul has a quality that everyone should be so lucky to have. It took Paul a lot of convincing that all the hard work was done previously, while we were learning about the various cultures, and that now was the time to celebrate that hard work. He still ate very little, although I knew he was starving.

These students have learned to work together; they have learned that they are a team. You can see the protection they have for each other in their interactions—when one is being disciplined, or if someone from the "outside" negatively infringes upon the group or its members. This support system is a very positive aspect in their lives. Each student has made some kind of personal accomplishment, some smaller than others, but an accomplishment nonetheless.

Our students have been given opportunities to experience things they have never experienced before (the ocean, other lifestyles and times, choices in their education, to be wrong and find their own right answers). They have been treated as individuals, have tasted success (metaphorically and literally), and have been encouraged and praised along the way. I feel that our accomplishments to date have been successful, and I am very proud of each and every student in Room 313A. And I wonder if every person who thinks that I am an intelligent young woman who is wasting her time or is crazy can sit back after a long day with a satisfied smile and say the same thing about his or her own job.[58]

At a cursory glance, you might say that Athena is indeed a "good" teacher, but as you look more carefully, you find examples of professional behaviors that have the potential to contribute over time to the professionalism that educators strive for—to care, to nurture, to act as a steward, to provide equal access to knowledge, and to respect the social context in which her students live. Athena clearly did not punch a time clock, she surely respected the diversity of the members of her class, she was reflective in her analysis of how her students were learning, she held professional knowledge that was rich in both content and pedagogical method, and she created an environment that was democratic and allowed each of the students voice and participation. At the end of the year she said, "This year the students were my supervisors and they made me earn my diploma." Perhaps that is what the principal of the high school meant when she said that the students at Bulkeley were helping to educate the next generation of teachers. But Athena did something else: she worked with others, both inside and outside her classroom, to establish an educational community.

As we watched Athena teach, we also saw how she struggled to make every lesson the very best it could be. We watched her question her own practice and professional character. We were proud to have been able to learn and work with a professional like Athena. We too grew through the numerous encounters we were privileged to have had with Athena, the teachers at Bulkeley, and the young people in the classrooms. Those on both sides of the professional fence were affected, and we think that the other fence—the one that keeps the school, the community, and the university apart—has been significantly weakened through the experience of partnership.

The Teacher's Responsibility
to Diverse Learners

*A progressive society counts individual variations as
precious since it finds in them the means of its own
growth. Hence a democratic society must, in consis-
tency with its ideal, allow for intellectual freedom and
the play of diverse gifts and interests in its educational
measures.*[1]

John Dewey

As the population in the United States becomes more diverse
in language, culture, and ethnicity, we add talent and variation as well as difficulties to the ever-changing role of the educational system. Teachers must be fully aware and accepting of the
changing population that they will be responsible for. A recent report by the Council of Economic Advisors for the President's Initiative on Race, *Changing America: Indicators of Social and Economic
Well-Being by Race and Hispanic Origin*, notes,

> The population of the United States is becoming in-
> creasingly diverse. In recent years, Hispanics and mi-
> nority racial groups—non-Hispanic blacks, Asians, and
> American Indians—have each grown faster than the
> population as a whole. In 1970 these groups together
> represented only 16 percent of the population. By 1998

this share had increased to 27 percent. Assuming current trends continue, the Bureau of the Census projects that these groups will account for almost half of the U.S. population by 2050.[2]

Equity and Diversity as Central Themes in Teacher Preparation

The educational implications of cultural pluralism attracted a good deal of attention in Western societies during the 1970s and 1980s, and they remain a matter of scholarly and professional concern. On grounds of equity and human rights, maximizing national talent, and maintaining social cohesion, these issues continue to exercise many societies. A curious feature, however, is that surprisingly little attention has been devoted to the social change potential of *teacher education*, despite its pivotal role in the initial preparation and continuing professional development of classroom practitioners, school inspectors, educational administrators and researchers.[3]

We would agree with Maurice Craft that teacher education programs must deliberately seek to make issues of equity and diversity central themes. Further, the relationship between diversity and equity in education, and the consequent access to knowledge for all, should be explored in many ways. A point that needs to be emphasized is that our conceptualization of diversity is somewhat broader than that sometimes found in the educational literature. Henry Louis Gates, Jr., summarizes this view of diversity in *Loose Canons: Notes on the Culture Wars*, which has been used to open the course "Multicultural Education: Equity and Excellence" in the University of Connecticut's teacher education program:

Ours is a late-twentieth-century world profoundly fissured by nationality, ethnicity, race, class, and gender. And the only way to transcend those divisions—to forge, for once, a civic culture that respects both differences and commonalties—is through education that seeks to comprehend the diversity of human culture. Beyond the hype and the high-flown rhetoric is a pretty homely truth: There is no tolerance without respect—and no respect without knowledge. Any human being sufficiently curious and motivated can fully possess another culture, no matter how "alien" it may appear to be.[4]

But certainly the goals of human understanding and tolerance are not fulfilled without considerable effort on the part of teacher educators in designing their programs. Course work, readings, and assignments in a preparation program need to address the diverse nature of today's school population. Issues such as the inclusion of students with disabilities in general education classrooms, gender equity, language preference, and multiculturalism in school and society must be emphasized. More important, these topics cannot be taught in isolation from the classroom; students must have concurrent opportunities to observe and work in a variety of clinical sites in order to confront the problems and issues they discuss in courses. Course work, clinical experience, and readings in the seminar all then converge to create a way of thinking that demonstrates understanding and acceptance of diversity. These combined activities push students to examine their own beliefs and attitudes, directly confronting issues such as equity, justice, truth, access to knowledge, and integration. Students learn that frequently there are no clear-cut or absolute answers—often a disquieting experience for anyone. Because these issues presented in course work are evident in their clinical placements, students realize the importance of taking the risks that may be associated with confronting them. Often these risks involve working with students who might otherwise be seen as "different." One student intern preparing to be a science teacher chose to work in an urban setting. She describes the experience in the following way: "Throughout this past year, I have learned numerous things that I believe will make me an excellent teacher and person. In addition to having learned various teaching methodologies and networking skills, I have also learned the appreciation of diversity and the importance of seeing individuals for what is on the inside, not for their exterior appearances."[5]

In *Teaching to Transgress: Education as the Practice of Freedom*, bell hooks stresses the need for practical experience in multicultural settings: "Among educators there has to be an acknowledgment that any effort to transform institutions so that they reflect a multicultural standpoint must take into consideration the fears teachers have when asked to shift their paradigms. There must be training sites where teachers have the opportunity to express those concerns while also learning to create ways to approach the multicultural classroom and curriculum."[6] At the University of Connecticut, all education students, regardless of final area of certification, have experiences spanning elementary through high school, have at least one urban placement, and work with students with disabilities. Students often spend time working with school principals, librarians, media specialists, parent and community groups, school social workers, guidance counselors, and other participants in the schooling process. Initially, teacher education students are placed in settings different from those in which they will ultimately teach. This configuration of placements is intentional and provides students with a variety of experiences across grade levels and areas of specialization. Prospective high school teachers spend one day a week for an entire semester in an elementary classroom, and future regular education teachers work in special education settings. Similarly, those who intend to be special educators spend at least two of these six clinical placements in regular education settings.

The series of diverse clinical experiences in partnership schools is vital to students' gaining insight and skill as multicultural educators. The ties between what they gain working in these settings and what they give back to the schools address directly the renewal of schools and the need to prepare new teachers in renewing environments. One intern who coordinated a large, schoolwide tutoring program provides personal evidence that the notion of simultaneous renewal is working:

> I believe I have benefited from my School of Education experience in its entirety. Before committing myself to being a teacher, I was very shy and unsure of myself. In working at various schools throughout my collegiate journey, I have grown to be professionally assertive, punctual, understanding, and dedicated. My experience at Bulkeley High School has embedded these characteristics deep within my personality. I have dealt with frustrations of parents and teachers and have done my best to reassure them that it is UConn's goal to help as much as possible. We are there to make the lives of the teachers a little easier, and I believe we have done so. Both my partner and I have been complimented for our tutoring with such statements as, "If you guys weren't there to help, I don't know where these students would be." It is statements such as this that make all the little frustrations worthwhile.[7]

In addition to course content and experiential learning in the clinical sites, issues of diversity should be addressed often and in considerable depth in seminar settings. As we suggested in Chapter Three, future educators must spend significant time conversing about racial and other matters that are potentially troublesome. Marilyn Cochran-Smith stresses this point: "As teacher educators attempt to open the unsettling discourse of race in the pre-service curriculum, they need to examine how this discourse and its implications for particular schools, communities, and classrooms are constructed and interpreted."[8]

As students begin to ask questions of themselves and their future colleagues in this regard, they form new hypotheses and propose alternatives, moving from an initial stage to more thoughtful and informed reflection, thereby developing a deeper understanding of the many social, cultural, and linguistic barriers facing today's school population. It is important for teacher educators to remember that they "must acknowledge the difficulty in helping adults to change entrenched and relatively unconscious habits of thought."[9] One of the tools that we have found helpful in this regard is the use of journals in gathering field notes, which in turn direct the discussion of inequity and prejudice. The students share their journal entries with the seminar leader, who responds in ways that encourage and support further reflection and analysis. These written dialogues often serve as the basis for conversations during the seminar, especially when several students identify similar themes.

During the seminar, students suggest background reading, and they lead discussions. Sessions might focus on teacher expectations and diverse student populations, homelessness and access to knowledge, integration and inclusion of students with disabilities, or excellence and equity. As students progress through the program, the discussions typically move from observations based on personal experience and opinion to conversations informed by their practice and literature. Assigned seminar readings are selected to push the conversation among seminar participants further into issues of diversity, within both the classroom and the community. Readings that we have found useful have been *Savage Inequalities* (1991) and *Amazing Grace* (1996), by Jonathan Kozol; *Schooling Homeless Children* (1994), by Sharon Quint; *Framing Dropouts* (1991), by Michelle Fine; *The Challenge to Care in Schools* (1992), by Nel Noddings; *There Are No Children Here* (1991), by Alex Kotlowitz; *Do We Have the Will to Educate All Children?* (1991), by Asa Hilliard; *Billy* (1993), by Albert French; *The Education of Little Tree* (1976), by Forrest Carter; *Selected Poems of Langston Hughes* (1959, reprinted 1990), by Langston Hughes; *Bastard Out of Carolina* (1992), by Dorothy Allison; *Pedagogy of the Oppressed* (1970) and *Pedagogy of Hope* (1992), by Paulo Freire; *Women's Ways of Knowing* (1986), by Mary Field Belenky, Blythe McVicker Clinchy, Nancy Rule Goldberger, and Jill Tarule; *Between Voice and Silence* (1995), by Jill McLean Taylor, Carol Gilligan, and Amy Sullivan; and *Angela's Ashes* (1996), by Frank McCourt.

One of the interns in the University of Connecticut's teacher education program spent a portion of her internship working in London in a partnership, and reflected on her experience in juxtaposition to another seminar reading, *The Moral Dimensions of Teaching,* edited by John Goodlad, Roger Soder, and Kenneth Sirotnik. In an e-mail response from London to her seminar group, the intern grappled with issues of diversity and one's own culture:

> Goodlad's point that schools are to nurture the young into the culture raises important questions. What is the "American" culture? Is it English-speaking, white Americans, most likely Protestant or maybe Catholic? Perhaps the best way for us to approach this point is to gain a decent education, not necessarily in a specialty, but a broad liberal arts background. But beyond book knowledge is experience. All of us in this seminar are gaining that through our internships in, most likely, far more diverse communities than we are from. In London, and in their schools, it is very diverse. I am in the city, and most cities are diverse. This allows us to experience, learn, and interact with other cultures. I am not sure what our responsibility as a teacher is in this area, but we must recognize that inherently we are teaching some "institutionalized" values because we will be working for an

institution. . . . We need to listen and to think through our own culture, morals, and values.[10]

Within the central theme of equity and diversity in teacher inquiry and reflection, we have identified four subthemes or commitments: to urban education, to gender equity, to linguistic diversity, and to inclusive educational practices.

A Commitment to Urban Education

Closely related to our concern with diversity, broadly conceived, must be a commitment to urban education. In the case of the University of Connecticut, three of the eight partnership districts with which we work are in culturally diverse urban communities characterized by many of the usual challenges and problems that face urban schools throughout the country. Our involvement in these urban schools has been beneficial not only to our students and faculty but to the teachers and students with whom we work. One of the encouraging elements of our collaboration has been the support that our teacher education program has received from teachers and administrators in these urban school districts. Most important, though, is the effect that working in an urban district has had on students preparing to be teachers, evidenced in the reflections of one of the master's interns working at Bulkeley High School in Hartford: "In reflecting on this year as a whole, I have developed greatly as a teacher and a person. Exposure to some of the problems that urban centers face brought . . . a better understanding of the challenges and roles that a teacher must assume in working with these students."[11]

Another student who worked in the same high school wrote about his internship experience of coordinating a large tutoring program and how this experience influenced his thinking about students in the city:

So much of this world tells the student that s/he cannot succeed, or, that s/he is not supposed to succeed. I doubt if I would have had such perseverance if I had to face the onslaught of negative expectations that many of these students face day in and out . . . where so many things attempt to suppress the inner-city student. This internship has solidified [my understanding of] the need to give each student whatever is necessary in order to succeed.[12]

Understanding and accepting diverse student populations also transcends the individual and requires an awareness of diverse communities and schools. Three examples come from the final inquiry projects conducted by interns working in an urban high school. Excerpts from their project introductions illustrate their concern for the individual as well as the broader school and community:

Those of us who are not familiar with an urban high school . . . are quick to realize that we have entered into a different world. Our preconceived ideas and our general frame of reference come into contact with reality. Our evaluations and perspective of the social setting that we encounter begin to become transformed. As an individual spends time in this world, he/she begins to understand the culture of an urban high school and those individuals who are part of this culture.[13]

Children in urban areas face many problems in all aspects of their lives—family, school, job, etc. They grow accustomed to failure both in and out of school. As educators, we can provide a route to success and guide our students down that route. There are many issues working against these children. We need to take a closer look and take action where we do have control, where we can make a difference in these young lives.[14]

Children in urban settings face many obstacles in obtaining a quality education. Oftentimes, the school has limited resources and outdated technology. Students often lack positive role models in their lives. School is often viewed as a place where "time has to be served." As educators, it is paramount that we teach our students the benefits of a quality education, and through education, we must teach students to advocate for themselves. Once armed with knowledge, students can begin to overcome the many obstacles facing them.[15]

Teachers in urban schools have consistently said that their own commitment to urban education has been reinforced and strengthened by the commitment of the university and its students. One teacher told us, "I think that there are a lot of things that the inner city doesn't have, and I think that UConn adds that little extra that maybe the kids otherwise wouldn't have: the added attention, the extra hands, the tutoring. It wouldn't exist without the partnership. No one in the school would [have the time] to organize such a massive scheduling. It just wouldn't happen, and kids would be falling through the cracks. My kids would have never seen a computer."[16]

A significant number of the interns designed their inquiry projects to examine issues that teachers and students regularly face in urban schools—for example: the myriad reasons that students leave high school, programs designed to assist students in at-risk situations, and teachers who succeed as outstanding educators in this environment. The titles of these inquiry projects are revealing:

- "A Qualitative Study of a Dropout Prevention Program and Its Effects on Students in an Urban High School Who Are At-Risk"

- "Portrayal of a Teacher in an Urban High School"

- "'At-Risk' in High School: Comparative Case Studies of Two Study Skills Populations"

- "The Role of the Discipline Policy in the Relationship Between Faculty and Students in an Urban High School"

- "An Urban High School Tutorial Program: The Effect on Student Achievement, Attendance, Attitude and Self-Esteem"

Collectively, these strong commitments to urban education have significantly changed the lives of future teachers; experience coupled with reflection and knowledge is strong indeed. One of us wrote in 1993: "I see caring and helping interactions between our university students, most of whom have never been in cities before, and I see wonderfully diverse students. I listen to our students struggle as their beliefs and understandings change and as their anger grows because of the callousness and injustice they see surrounding city life. They can never be the same."[17]

A Commitment to Gender Equity

Exploring women's relationships with other women and girls, as well as women's relationships with men and boys, leads us to ask how and whether these relationships can be or become transformative, be more effective in working toward a just and caring society and in preventing systematic as well as personal injustice, neglect, violation, and violence.[18]

The commitment to gender equity, broadly conceived, is a topic often given short shrift in programs preparing future teachers. It may be that those designing programs have little understanding of or sympathy toward matters pertaining to gender equity. Too, students themselves are often reluctant to discuss openly the role that gender plays in the educational process.[19] Patricia Campbell and Jo Sanders remind us that although "researchers and program developers have produced a steady output on gender equity in education, . . . gender equity in teacher education has received much less attention" in course work or textbooks.[20]

We find quite troublesome the reluctance of our students to engage fully in discussions relative to gender and gender equity.

Although a small number of inquiry projects have examined gender as a variable in learning, and although we have found a few instances of written reflection on the subject, for the most part discussions of issues of gender are markedly absent. We are therefore increasing our focus on gender, through readings and subsequent conversation, in our teacher education courses. Thus, even when the reading of books such as *Women's Ways of Knowing* causes uneasy reactions, we have found that pushing further discussion in conjunction with clinical experience is beginning to pay off. For example, following the reading of *Women's Ways of Knowing,* an intern working in an urban high school struggled with issues of gender and race and how the students in her classroom have chosen to configure themselves. She wrote,

> No way will it [sexism or racism] ever happen in my classroom. I won't stand for it—yet it does. How is it that in a class with five women and three men that the men end up dominating the scenes they are near? Sure, a certain amount of it is situational. With eight people and five computers, someone is going to have to pair up. Girls pair up with boys and a pattern emerges. Boys and girls flirt, boys avoid doing the work, yet they end up with the power to make the content choices. For some reason this does not sit well with me. Add to this another part of the equation. The male population is entirely Hispanic, as are two of the girls. Two other girls are African American, and one other girl is Dominican. . . . [In the end the boys dominate and the girls from different ethnic groups do not work together.] This especially concerns me because these students travel in a [special education] cluster. They have many of the same classes. . . . An option would be to segregate them, but I don't think this would address the real issues here of racism and gender.[21]

Another intern examined issues of racism and sexism in a journal entry after reading bell hooks's *Teaching to Transgress*:

> bell hooks's book *Teaching to Transgress* addresses the issue of black feminism in our society. She criticizes the educational structure and practices of American education as well as her own education in South Africa. The racism and sexism she has experienced through her years as a student and teacher have shaped her thinking and reflection of education. "I begin to interrogate the ways in which racist and sexist biases shaped and informed all scholarship dealing with black experience, with female experience" (hooks, p. 121). As a future educator, it is important to realize the biases inherent in our culture and therefore our educational practices.[22]

Inquiry projects that the master's interns conducted also indicate some concern about how gender and gender equity affect their role as educators and the educational lives of their students. Two of these inquiry projects were entitled: "English Teachers' Perceptions of Gender-Related Writing Differences" and "Differences in Self-Efficacy on Computer Tasks Between Genders."

A Commitment to Linguistic Diversity

As the percentage of non-English-speaking students in the public schools continues to grow, it will become increasingly important for classroom teachers to be familiar with issues of language and language variation, especially as such issues bear on student learning. Teacher education programs by and large overlook this significant area, assuming that the needs of non-English-speaking students will be met by specially trained professionals (bilingual educators and teachers of English as a second language, for example). In addition, the idioms of the daily lives of many students who speak English as a first language are often distinct from those found in standard English.[23] Because language and its use represent power in this and many other countries,[24] it is critical that teachers be fully cognizant of public policy in the field of bilingual education and its effect on access to equal educational rights. One of us connects language rights to the right to education:

> Teachers should be not merely recipients of educational language policies. They should be directly involved in the development, implementation, and evaluation of such policies. Language policies inevitably reflect social, economic, and political agendas; they require the teacher to be aware of and sensitive to issues of power, equity, and justice. Finally, teachers should be aware of and sensitive to issues of language rights as a component of both human rights and educational rights.[25]

We suggest that traditional approaches to educating students with language diversity are not complex enough to meet the wide variety of linguistic needs of the student population. Teacher education programs must ensure that their graduates have a basic knowledge of applied linguistics, including language acquisition, language variation and diversity, second-language learning, and clinical linguistics.[26] We believe an understanding of all of these subjects is necessary in teacher education and, further, that a combination of clinical experience, cultural understanding, and in-depth analyses of the factors involved in language learning is critical to the commitment to linguistic diversity that teachers must have. An example of the extent to which this can be done comes directly from one of the University of Connecticut interns. It illustrates how language diversity played a key role in his work, in his commitment to diversity in language and culture, and consequently in his culminating inquiry project.

Rick Abrams, a future elementary, special education, and English teacher, chose to complete his year-long internship at Hartford's Bulkeley High School, where an overwhelming majority of the students speak Spanish as their first language. Having never before been in an inner-city high school (he grew up on a farm in Massachusetts) and not speaking any Spanish, Rick wondered many things, among them: how difficult is it for students to learn in a language that is not their own, and more specifically, would immersion in another language be a successful method for learning a second language? He sought advice and assistance from a bilingual history teacher from Puerto Rico who was teaching at Bulkeley and from a professor at the university specializing in language learning and linguistics.

Rick spent one period every day learning Spanish by becoming a student himself in Ramon Vega's bilingual history class, taught almost entirely in Spanish; thus, Rick's language was in the minority. Rick, acting as a participant-observer, conducted his research on his own learning. Throughout this process, he kept extensive field notes on his experience—for example:

> I consider myself a sample of my study; I immersed myself in this class. I even became a student . . . worked on the same projects they did. I tried to get the sense of what it is like to be a bilingual student. Without my notes, without those reflections as they happened—I mean, if I didn't write things down as soon as they happened—my project would have been lost. My project would have had no credibility, would have had no force, would have had no authenticity. My inquiry project was the most important thing I did.[27]

In his final write-up of the inquiry project, Rick discussed at great length the difficult and often-frustrating process of learning a second language as an adult. In the end, he learned quite a bit of Spanish but not enough to have been a successful student in the high school history class; he did not receive a high grade in this class. Some of Rick's related insights help us understand the significant impact that exposure to different cultures and languages can have on those preparing to be teachers and how reflection and inquiry play key roles in this process:

> I enjoyed Ramon's class so much, in fact, I eventually found myself attending it every day. I wanted to become bilingual. Eventually, however, what began as a selfish motivation turned into intrigue over the overwhelming problems these students faced. This involvement ultimately turned into my research project. I conducted an ethnographic study in which I became the participant-observer in the class, in order to get at what it is like to be a LEP [limited English proficiency] Puerto Rican high school student in a mainland school. The project met with mixed success . . . it was unlike any experience I have ever had. . . . The "inquiry project" yielded some sixty pages of writing, of which I am very proud. To this day I take it out from time to time and leaf through it and find myself somewhat in awe of what I had accomplished.[28]

Finally, Rick told us the real importance of his inquiry into social and linguistic barriers: "These are kids. I think our society emphasizes what makes us different when what binds us together as human beings is so much more important. What makes us similar, across ethnic and racial boundaries is so much more important. These are kids with dreams and hopes and every bit as capable as I was at their age. We're talking about human beings who deserve the chance to try to fulfill their dreams just like anybody else."[29]

Other student inquiry projects give evidence of the commitment to linguistic and cultural diversity:

- "Ways to Improve Bilingual Education"

- "Multicultural Education in an Inner-City High School"

- "Exploring Relationships Between Culture and Motivation in the ESL Classroom"

- "Exploring Nontraditional Methods of Teaching Second Language Acquisition That Best Motivate Student Learning"

- "Cultural Difference in the Classroom"

Going beyond required course work and assignments to explore these matters in depth has given future teachers a stronger and more personal understanding of how critical a student's language and culture are to access to knowledge.

A Commitment to the Inclusion of Students with Disabilities

Although "the greater integration of special and general education is an educational development long overdue," according to John Goodlad, "effecting it stirs and rearranges an extraordinary political, economic, and educational network of agencies, institutions, and individuals. . . . Significant change affects entire ecosystems, arousing passions, changing human behaviors, and exposing reefs not marked on any charts."[30]

Preparing teachers for inclusive education is as much a matter of attitudes and moral responsibility as it is of knowledge and skill. There is much discussion about inclusion of students with disabilities and the need to create more accommodating educational settings, yet traditional perceptions and attitudes about what a teacher's job is (for both general and special educators) obstruct the fuller inclusion of students with disabilities. As a result, many students continue to be placed in special education settings for significant portions of their schooling. If educators are to be successful in challenging these continuing practices of segregation, then the belief that individuals with disabilities can and should be fully integrated into the school community must become widespread. John Goodlad and Thomas Lovitt noted in *Integrating General and Special*

Education, "Although the mission of enculturating all is at the core a moral one, it is now defined in part by legal terms. There are no legitimate arguments for denying access to knowledge. The educational environments provided in schools are to be minimally restrictive and maximally educative."[31]

As educational institutions rethink how schools are structured and instruction is delivered, schools of education must simultaneously redesign preparation programs to match and participate in these changing cultures. All teachers must become the focus of these changes. But we are challenged in this regard by the separation of curriculum and experiences still found in many "regular" and "special" education teacher preparation programs. Clearly, the practice of separating instructional systems for students with and without disabilities has been perpetuated by the unconnected teacher preparation programs currently found in most colleges and universities across the country.[32] It is not surprising, then, that regular education teachers resist integrating children with special learning needs into their classrooms and that special education teachers are equally resistant to changing their perceived job roles. Goodlad and Field state,

> All of this suggests a system that is failing to adequately prepare teachers to meet the educational needs of students with disabilities. It also suggests a sense of separateness between students, professors, and programs in institutions of higher education engaged simultaneously in preparing teachers for both general and special assignments in schools. Undoubtedly, this separation contributes to the separateness of general and special education in this nation's schools. Clearly, there is ample room for closer collaboration and a greater degree of integration.[33]

Teacher educators must be willing to work with one another if programs are to model collaboration for future teachers. They must set out a course of study that exemplifies this type of collaboration and provides students with appropriate experiences with a diversity of learners. Most beginning students in a teacher education program are set upon a career path. They come to the program intending to be first-grade teachers, high school mathematics teachers, and so on. At the University of Connecticut, students have their first clinical experiences outside their intended area of certification. At the outset of the program, many of the students protest that they did not "sign up to be special education teachers." During the early stages of the program, they often misunderstand the sequence of clinical placements that takes them outside their intended area of teaching. Yet as they gain experience with a variety of grades and types of learners, they feel less afraid and unprepared. One student elaborates:

> I was lucky enough to be placed in a special education classroom for my clinical experience last year. Due to this, I felt that I was one step ahead in understanding the importance of the special needs of special education students. [This] clinical experience offered me a chance to apply the knowledge that I learned in Exceptionality I, because they were in the same semester. . . . I believe that it is very beneficial for an education major to gain special education experience prior to becoming a teacher. . . . [34]

Another student told us,

> I think one of the real strengths of this program is how it tests your ability to adapt and the way it throws you into situations that you never anticipated. . . . The first clinical experience I had was in a resource room for high school students. There was a boy who had severe cerebral palsy and a girl who had Down syndrome. I was scared to death because I went into the program focusing

on elementary education. I wasn't interested in special education or in working with special needs kids—or at least I didn't think I was. It was one of the most incredible experiences of my life. Talk about reflective practice—stepping back and thinking about what I was actually doing was just unbelievable.[35]

In their first year of the University of Connecticut's program, students from across teaching disciplines and grade levels take their first core course on exceptionality. Students are exposed to history and laws, characteristics of exceptional learners, and teacher responsibility for the inclusion of students with disabilities. This course asks students to confront their own attitudes toward persons with disabilities as well as stereotypes about these learners. At the conclusion of the course, students reflect on the most important things they learned. They have responded that: "not all 'special children' need to be separated from the mainstream class" and that "as a teacher I need to adjust to individual needs." They have indicated that their understanding of "laws, guidelines, and parent, child, and teacher rights (and responsibilities)" increased and "that all children learn differently and should be considered when one prepares a lesson, test, or other assignment." They made it clear that "people are people first; the handicap is secondary" and that "attitude matters and makes a difference in the classroom." As another way of evaluating this core course, students are asked to describe their attitude toward having a student with a disability in their classroom. Overwhelmingly, they responded that they would be "accepting," "enthusiastic," "eager," and "optimistic." They stated that the experience of having a student with a disability in their classroom would be "exciting," "challenging," "rewarding," and "heartwarming." The following three excerpts from statements of philosophy relative to the inclusion of students with disabilities are illustrative:

> I believe that all students should be allowed into general education classrooms to gain a wider range of experience. It is not fair to exclude these students because of a disability.[36]

> I believe that education should allow people to participate in American society to the best of their abilities. As a future educator, I support the legal provisions that support teaching and instruction designed to improve the education of all students.[37]

> Inclusion, when offered with the appropriate level of resources and help, is the . . . ideal educational setting. For me, the inclusionary school is the last defense against a total loss of community spirit. Inside an inclusive classroom, equity is in its finest form. It offers an umbilical connection to a better society, and it is up to me and my contemporaries to further this vision.[38]

In their second year of preparation, students take a subsequent course on exceptionality that addresses curriculum and instructional practices and the need for collaboration. The course activities and assignments are designed to correlate with work that students are undertaking in specific pedagogical courses. Cooperative activities in which students learn to depend on each other's expertise are often included. Secondary students work in groups of four or five to develop interdisciplinary units of study. During the course, these groups of students are joined by colleagues preparing to be special educators. Together they plan instructional modifications that can be integrated into each of the interdisciplinary units.

In the master's (internship) year, students integrate all of their previous experiences and expand their roles to include being teacher-leaders and researchers. As interns, students become immersed in the culture of the school, spending twenty hours per week in this clinical placement for the entire school year and taking on roles with responsibility for the larger school community. The interns often step outside their areas of certification to work on projects in which students with special education needs are the primary focus.

An intern whose certification area is elementary education worked with a colleague in special education in a middle school math and writing lab for students with special needs: "I taught computer-based lessons. . . . I took this assignment because I wanted to get a background in technology, but also because I wanted to learn more about special education and get a flavor and sensitivity for the role of the special educator. This year was a tremendous learning experience for me."[39]

Through experiences and course work, teachers-to-be have gained an understanding and willingness to plan and modify curriculum and instruction for a wide variety of students. One future mathematics teacher had this to say about his internship year working in a computer lab for high school students with disabilities:

> The experience I gained working with special education students is something I will value once I begin teaching in my regular classroom. I had to make various modifications to my methods of instruction to accommodate the needs of the students. For example, one of my students was an extremely poor reader and could not read the instructions that came with every lesson. Therefore, I wrote the directions using the Simple Text application on the computer and the student was able to hear the directions read aloud.[40]

A large number of the year-long inquiry projects during the master's year have dealt directly with students with disabilities—their inclusion in the mainstream of education as well as curriculum and instruction for these individuals—for example:

- "Writing to Understand: A Study on Integrating Process Writing and Computer Technology to Teach Writing to Students with Special Needs"

- "A Qualitative Study of the Use of Computers as a Tool for Students with Developmental Disabilities"

- "A Computer Lab's Effects on Special Education Students' Mathematical Abilities"

- "Prewriting: A Look at Computer-Based Metacognitive Skills and Their Effect on Inner-City Students with Learning Disabilities"

- "The Effects of Team Teaching and Mainstreaming on Regular and Special Education Students' Self-Efficacy Toward Learning and Social Academic Communication"

- "Collaboration Among Regular and Special Educators: An Ethnographic Study of a New Staff"

Some of the projects were conducted by students preparing to be special educators, and others have been undertaken by future elementary and secondary teachers.

Program faculty and students have kept extensive field notes. Embedded in these notes are comments that reflect programmatic as well as student change. One such story about student change gives a clear picture about the types of educators this program is committed to preparing. It opens and closes with observations by one of us:

David, a junior in the teacher preparation program intending to be a secondary English teacher, was assigned to a computer-based writing lab in the Hartford Professional Development Center. In this lab he was working with a group of special education students of whom approximately 60 percent were Hispanic. One of the students in this class was a young man named Mark with cerebral palsy. Mark has limited speech, poor motor control, and is in a wheelchair. David perceived Mark to be "retarded." Despite their educational, socioeconomic, cultural, and racial differences, these two young men began to work together, learning the computer, the software, and the writing process. A number of weeks later, Mark printed out the following story:

My Life Story

I was born . . . to Regina Perez and to a father I don't know about and have never met. I wonder what it would have been like to have had a father figure in my life. The reason why he left was because when I was two years old I was found to have Cerebral Palsy. My mom said times were hard when he left. She also said she wanted to give me up because the doctors told her that I was going to be retarded. But she didn't let that happen. It took a lot of years before I could actually walk. The first of many operations were performed. It was long and hard but I did what I had to do to achieve the first goal and my best goal I think. There are still a lot of obstacles I have to overcome. But I am determined to achieve all of my goals in life.

It was fascinating to watch these two young men who have forever affected each other's lives. As Mark says, "I'm not retarded—I wish all my teachers knew that," David and the school principal who are listening have tears in their eyes.[41]

David's life as a teacher has been forever altered as a result of his contact with Mark. In the future, David will be far less likely to base opinions about his students on casual observation or labels of disability. In fact, David went on to work toward dual certification—in English and special education.

Teachers Taking the Responsibility to Educate America's Children

The impact on future educators enrolled in teacher education programs designed to foster a spirit of inclusion and equity in the educational experience comes through in this newspaper article describing one graduate of such a program following two years of employment as a special educator at Kramer Middle School in Windham, Connecticut (one of the state's urban "priority"—most impoverished—school districts):

> When Pam Flaherty decided she wanted to be a teacher, she had no thought of teaching in an inner-city school. But her student teaching experience as a senior at the University of Connecticut changed her mind.
>
> And when faced with a choice of schools for her first teaching job, she jumped at the chance to work in an urban setting.
>
> Looking back, Flaherty recalls her shock when she was assigned to Hartford's Bulkeley High School as a student teacher after she had requested a suburban elementary school.
>
> "I had pigeonholed myself into the type of school I attended myself," she says. "If I had not been pushed at UConn to explore an urban school setting, I wouldn't have even given it a chance."[42]

During her final year of teacher preparation, this student had made the following comments about her experience at Bulkeley and the choice to work in urban schools:

> I never thought I would be successful teaching at the secondary level in an urban setting. On the contrary, I had always imagined that I would teach in a suburban

elementary school at the primary level. However, [a faculty member] believed in me when I had my share of doubts. As a result, I had a terrific student teaching experience in which I developed and expanded my teaching ability. The urban setting was both challenging and rewarding. In fact, I am now completing my master's internship placement in the same school.[43]

Voicing this same theme, Donna Miziasak, at the conclusion of her internship in the same urban high school, told us: "This year I really learned how things work. I'm not so idealistic either, saying things like 'I want to get the perfect job.' Now I can never look back and be like I was. I don't want some cushy job. I want a challenge. I want to work harder because that's what this program has made me want to do."[44]

We have also found strong evidence that future teachers can develop positive attitudes toward inclusive educational practice. During the final exam in a course on exceptionality, students are asked to write a case study of a student with a disability with whom they have interacted. The final question on the exam directs them to examine the classroom teacher's attitude toward the inclusion of the student in question and to examine their own attitude. A future secondary teacher answered in the following way:

> The teacher seems positive about having the student in the classroom. It is tiring, trying to be in so many places at one time, but the teacher realizes how important it is for the child to be there. Personally, I don't feel there is a question; this student belongs in the classroom. While it may be tiring and at times very tough, the student has to come first. Realistically, some days may be very, very long, but no one ever said teaching was easy. Diversity is important in the outside world, and it needs to be so within the classroom as well.[45]

Collectively, where have these future educators chosen to work? Jonathan Jette spent his first months following graduation teaching at a facility for youthful offenders and subsequently received a special education job; Donna Miziasak is working as a special educator in a state prison for adolescents; Ted Burkett is teaching in Turkey; Carrie Olah, Heather Westervelt-Vega, and Jennifer Malz, all of whom spoke little Spanish upon entering the program, are now fluent in the language and have chosen to work in schools where Spanish is the first language of the majority of the children (Jennifer spent a year teaching in Puerto Rico); Rick Abrams, who entered the program as an elementary education major, finished with certifications in elementary education, English education, and special education, is happily working with students with learning disabilities, but unhappy to be in a private school; Brian Keating is working in an urban alternative education program for adolescents as an English teacher; Donnah Rochester took her first year off to have a child; Dan Broderick was seeking employment as an elementary education teacher in New York City; Lorianne Brown completed her internship at Bulkeley High School in Hartford, plans to be an elementary educator, and is also considering advanced course work in counseling and school social work; Enzo Zocco, a graduate of the Hartford Public Schools, has taken a teaching job there; Jennifer Del Conte, an English educator, went on to complete a second master's degree in deaf education and a sixth year in special education; Athena Neilson, an English educator, chose from a variety of job offers to work at Windham High School, an urban school committed to serious restructuring; and many others have taken similar career paths.

There appear to be some clear patterns in the choices these individuals have made: to work with diverse student populations, to work in urban settings, and to look outside the classroom into the larger educative community. If you asked them about their commitment to equity in education, the need to provide equal access to knowledge, and the need for the community called school to be broader than it is traditionally conceived, they would more than likely agree with this colleague:

> When I look at our classroom, I feel I'm looking at a little microcosm of life. . . . The children here are more diverse than anyone can notice right off the bat. They are very diverse concerning their personal experiences and beliefs. One child is homeless, while another has a family and recently was given a coming-out party. One boy aspires to work for the phone company carrying wire, while another wants to go to college and "be something great." . . . They have all the ups and downs of the outside world, and yet there is the sanctuary created by the community of the teams—teams of kids, teams of teachers. Finding your community and being responsible to it is [part of] what democracy in education is all about.[46]

The words of Mary Catherine Bateson provide comfort to educators as they take on the uneasy challenge of living in others' homes, schools, and worlds: "Today I can see that even in our differences my mother [Margaret Mead] and I shared the struggle to combine multiple commitments, always liable to conflict or interruption. Each of us had to search in ambiguity for her own kind of integrity, learning to adapt and improvise in a culture in which we could only partly be at home."[47]

6

Enabling Teachers to Assume Leadership Roles

Significant educational change is needed if we are to provide equitable educational opportunities for all America's youth. Although the literature of education is replete with calls for the reform of our educational structure, these calls sometimes venture far from reality. Too often, reform suggestions focus on outside forces and do not look inside the classroom, where the teacher is the center—the force behind learning and consequently the true agent for educational change. Harnessing the energy and intelligence of the teacher is the essential first step in educational reform. Therefore, we must create a positive environment for teachers to teach in, and we must prepare educators who can assist in the creation of different educational structures. And further, the education of new professionals must be coupled with the reeducation of the existing teaching force. Linked together in the common purpose of teaching all children, educators in both public schools and institutions of higher education would have considerable influence: the power to create new schools in which learning is commonplace and failure is significantly reduced. For this to transpire, Thoreau's words directing us to action must not be taken lightly: "But, to speak practically and as a citizen, unlike those who call themselves no-government men, I ask for, not at once no government, but *at once* a better government. Let every man make known what kind of government would command his respect, and that will be one step toward obtaining it."[1] Teachers must make known the kind of school that "would command [their] respect." Teachers acting in professional ways will need to be the leaders of educational change.

Schooling, Democracy, and the "Ordinary" Citizen: Teachers as the Leaders of Change

In *The Moon Is Down* (1942), John Steinbeck asks readers to reflect on some basic yet testy questions. Among these not easily answered but requiring much thought are: How do the power of the community, the ideal of freedom, and a government run by and for the people act to prevent those who would take away democracy from doing so? Our question becomes: How might these lessons be applied to our efforts to change schooling? And further, how will consideration of these questions move teachers, as individuals and as groups, to take action, to resist the status quo, to become leaders? And, as teachers assume broader responsibilities, how do they become comfortable with being the dissenting voice?

Organizational Change: Teachers as Leaders

Recall our discussion of democracy and American public schooling and the close relationship between the two. As Robert Westbrook describes it: "The relationship between public schooling and democracy is a conceptually tight one. Schools have become one of the principal institutions by which modern states reproduce themselves, and insofar as those states are democratic, they will make use of schools to prepare children for democratic citizenship." But Westbrook cautions us that "American democracy is now weak and its prospects are dim. The anemia of public life in the United States— a polity in which even such minimal practices of citizenship as voting do not engage many Americans—is reflected in public schooling that, despite lip service to education for democratic citizenship, has devoted few resources or even much thought to its requirements."[2]

Connecting this discussion of democracy to the role of schools in socializing citizens who are able and willing to participate in this form of governance challenges us to move beyond the usual rhetoric of school restructuring. In other words, it directs us to move our thinking about schooling, the classroom, and curriculum to a different plane. It forces us to consider individual freedom in relation to the common good. It requires that we address issues of equity and diversity. And it compels us to answer Walter Parker's question: "How can people live together justly, in ways that are mutually satisfying, and that leave our differences, both individual and group, intact and our multiple identities recognized?"[3]

What, then, are the multiple roles of the professional educator? Of course, the teacher is first and foremost a teacher—directly responsible for the educational development of so many young minds and souls. We are all aware of the daily influence that a teacher has on his or her pupils to direct learning, to make children laugh or cry, to teach them to learn on their own, to create an environment that is caring, and so much more. But as teachers take on the mantel of stewards, they assume distinctive characteristics enabling them to move beyond the classroom, to influence the manner in which the educational environment is arranged. A future special educator explains,

> I did spend a good deal of time working with the school principal on various projects that were indirectly related to my internship [assisting teaching teams in developing, implementing, and evaluating interdisciplinary curricular units]. I worked on the Title I budget and the School Improvement Plan. Interdisciplinary curriculum funding and support were included in both. What was more important was the experience. By working with the principal, I was able to see how the school works from a different perspective. I feel that I have a greater appreciation for what it takes to effectively run a school.[4]

Yet many educators are not afforded such sustained opportunities to learn to be leaders. They continue to find themselves in bureaucracies rather than in environments that foster reflective practice and teacher inquiry—both essential if teachers are to be leaders of change. Here it is important to look at how Kenneth Sirotnik differentiates between what he calls "understanding" and "informed understanding." Critical inquiry envelops the ability to reflect earnestly and critically on the meaning and activities of teaching, enabling the teacher to make informed and rational decisions about his or her classroom practice. Self-critique and reflection is crucial to the self-evaluative process in that "it poses both the current and historical context for issues and problems, it suggests the data to inform the process, and it demands explicit consideration of the often hidden values and human interests guiding educational practices."[5]

However, the actual conditions of schooling provide little support for reflection and critical inquiry.[6] Schools operate in the midst of tensions resulting from the clash between a historically entrenched bureaucratic model and an evolving professional model of teaching. The bureaucratic model represents an attempt to minimize uncertainty in the workplace and standardize working conditions. It emphasizes routinizing the work of teachers and to some extent favors generic curriculum packages, which inevitably—and by some accounts deliberately—constrain the decision making of teachers.[7] Such bureaucratic forms of control trivialize teaching tasks, turning teaching into a series of "rule-based checklists."[8] The emerging professional model, in contrast, treats the uncertainty of teacher practice as a given and concentrates on aiding the educator's decision making in the face of uncertain conditions.[9] Reflective practice is far more compatible with the professional than the bureaucratic model of teaching.

The uncertain conditions under which teachers make decisions arise as a result of three major factors: (1) student needs are variable and constantly in flux; (2) teachers serve an interactive group as opposed to individual clients; and (3) the goals and purposes given to teachers are ambiguous, multiple, and at times contradictory.[10] Sharon Conley contends that today's teacher acts "as a constrained decision maker" who "deals with uncertainty by weighing alternatives and taking creative risks, while at the same time being aware that he or she is operating within a specific organizational context characterized by goals, norms, precedents, and colleagues."[11]

Curricular Change: Teachers Resisting the Status Quo

Could we ever have guessed that Edward would lean over to Sharon during a reading of *The Rime of the Ancient Mariner* and whisper, "It feels like the ghost of the ancient mariner is in this room right now. Do you think he's here? Do you?" Until Christmas, Edward had hardly spoken to us. He was so withdrawn from others that he often buried his face in the hood of his kangaroo shirt and rocked back and forth during lessons and class meetings. He seldom wrote, preferring to sit by himself and draw minutely detailed mazes of miniature battle scenes, seemingly obsessed with blood dripping from gaping wounds and vicious swords. On a blustery January day, Coleridge's words had reached across time and space to touch a little boy who wanted, for the very first time, to talk to his teachers about the world inside his head. The next day, he picked up the conversation again. "Do you know," he told us, "that an imagination is a terrible thing? The pictures in my mind really, really scare me." For Edward, the thing that had frightened him most—his ability to conjure detailed, vivid images—became the vehicle through which he was able, for the first time that we could see, to connect with others in the classroom.[12]

The insights chronicled by Edward's teachers, Patricia Clifford and Sharon Friesen, illustrate the vulnerability of children and thus how critical relevant curriculum becomes. Unfortunately, as Marleen C. Pugach and Cynthia L. Warger note, "The concern for personal relevance is one that has been lacking in both special and general education, where the acquisition of skills, basic or otherwise, in the absence of meaningful context has been the norm."[13] Nel Noddings warns that educational responses to the need for "deep social change" have been all too "shallow" and that we must "recognize and admit that curriculum content—in the form of traditional subjects—has never been a big contributor to satisfaction with schooling."[14] What does seem to matter here is the connection between the content of the curriculum and pedagogical nurturing. Kristi Maynard, whose work in interdisciplinary curriculum as an intern led her to assist the entire school, believes that these connections—between disciplines and between the student, the teacher, and the lessons being learned—are of great importance:

> I have found that I have internalized interdisciplinary thought. . . . The research I have done and the experiences I have had this year have allowed me to see the importance of making connections between disciplines as well as making learning authentic and useful. As adults, when do we ever use the disciplines separately in our lives? Almost never. When do we strive to learn something and to do our best? When what we are learning is something that is useful to us or something that we are interested in. We need to make learning important to our students. I believe that interdisciplinary curriculum allows all these things to happen because it allows students to see connections between disciplines, how what they are learning might be useful to them and provide interesting thematic anchors for them.[15]

Like organizational change, curricular change will be influenced by both individuals and the communities in which they live and work. Conversations on this question may be pivotal as teachers and their administrators open discussion about what is important for students in a given classroom, school, or community to learn. These dialogues would best be about "wondering and worrying together—deliberating—about how we ought to live together."[16]

But as we sink more deeply into the quicksand of the standards movement and the assessment frenzy, we may find ourselves further away from, rather than closer to, meeting the educational and emotional needs of all—of having conversation that is collaborative, of providing equitable access to knowledge, of addressing the need to care in schools. David Imig is most concerned about the dilemma that educators face as they try to balance the demands of standards and the moral dimensions of the profession. In commenting on Massachusetts's present view of teacher competence, which is based on assessment of general knowledge and little or no connection to reflection or the moral dimensions of teaching, he alerts educators and teacher educators that the sand is deepening and widening simultaneously and that they must be watchful and recommit themselves to the moral principles of the profession. In the absence of commitment, curricula for future teachers and children alike will trap them in narrow ways of thinking and acting.

> As I participated in John Goodlad's series of meetings for the National Network for Educational Renewal in Seattle in early August [1998], I was struck by how different the world views of teacher educators are on accountability. Goodlad engaged participants from 33 colleges and universities in four days of conversation on the moral underpinnings of their program and their commitment to preparing teachers for a political democracy. The focus was on capacity building and leadership development, engaging prospective teachers in the human conversation, and sharing scholarship and best practices.[17]

Edward, it is worth noting, was in Patricia Clifford's and Sharon Friesen's combined first/second-grade classroom in Calgary, Alberta, Canada. Although he was only in the early grades, Edward was exposed by his knowledgeable and caring teachers to the *Rime of the Ancient Mariner* as well as "stories and films about Columbus, Leonardo da Vinci, Genghis Khan, the Arthurian saga, outer space, Greek myths, and Chinese legends."[18] We wonder how many teachers would find Coleridge's story within the curricular competencies thrust upon them as first- or second-grade teachers? Not nearly enough, we fear. This state of curricular affairs brings us full circle to the need for teachers to be intellectuals, to be reflective in their practice, to nurture through their own pedagogical practice those in their care. Teachers who have a depth of knowledge in both pedagogy and the arts and sciences will be more capable of taking part in the construction and review of curriculum standards. And they will have strength to resist the status quo.

Professional Preparation: The Moral Dimensions in Action

We believe that the type of professional preparation explored in this book can encourage teachers to act professionally and put into their daily practice the moral dimensions of their profession. The following four stories (excerpts from longer versions) give evidence to our belief that there remains an altruism and dedication among those choosing to become teachers. Future educators understand the moral implications of their chosen profession; they can be and are reflective about their work; and they respect diversity and are willing and able to confront this diversity within their classrooms and schools. These stories provide examples of leaders who can take action: action in the analysis of their teaching, action in confronting their individual fears, action in curricular change, and action in confronting the system.

Preparing Future Citizens: The Teacher's Influence

The first story is by Sara Kaplan, who at the time of its writing was preparing to be a social studies teacher. During her internship year, she worked with a history teacher, Steve Morrell (who had also served as her cooperating teacher during student teaching the previous year). For a number of years, Morrell had been committed to helping students from Bulkeley High School in Hartford experience the world. Sara spent the year assisting him in the creation and implementation of a Russian studies curriculum that culminated in a journey to Moscow. We have chosen entries from her journal and several profiles of her students to illustrate how the study of another culture can prepare citizens of our own country and the world.

A Journey to Moscow and Back

It is December 9, 1993. I am an intern at Bulkeley High School in Hartford, Connecticut. But "Where am I?" is a question I have found difficult to answer. I may be in the conference room learning Russian. I may be in the library helping a student figure out a Stalinist joke. . . . Maybe I am not even at Bulkeley. I am at Yale or the University of Connecticut or a Russian immigrant's house learning about Russia. I might be looking at the Pulaski statue downtown, thinking of how similar it looks to the Peter the Great statue in St. Petersburg. I am learning, growing, and making a difference for a small but significant population at Bulkeley High School. That is where I am.

My role at BHS is to facilitate my students' learning about Russia. The method is individualized. Good readers are presented with the opportunity to read Marx's *Communist Manifesto,* the complete version. Good interpreters study photos or cartoons to detect Russian attitudes toward leaders. Listeners hear music by Tchaikovsky and Shostakovich. . . . All students discuss the impact of Shostakovich's sound on the Russian collective memory of Stalin. Some students know the name of the crescendo—others can hum it. . . . In general, my students' learning methods are as varied as the above description of my typical day at BHS. My role has expanded from "Russian studies tutor" to "Russian studies program coordinator." In this role, I work to reach out of the normal confines of teaching to make learning real and applicable.

Carol and Bryan discussed religion this week. Carol discussed her religious revelations when she traveled to see the Pope. She said that people need some religion, especially to help them get through the bad times. How can people get through problems if they do not feel spiritual support? She stated a theme that many people point to as a reason for the demise of the USSR. The nation denied religion. What helped people believe in a better tomorrow?

Student profile: M.B., female, age 17, grade 12, ethnicity: Romanian, activity: cheerleading, proud of her two-year transition from the New Arrival Program to mainstream academic classes, hopes to be a lawyer. M.B. left Romania two years ago. Therefore, I assumed that she already had an adequate understanding of the Soviet system. By the end of October, I realized that her understanding of the Soviet system was vague and hardly helpful. She lived during a period of tumultuous change as Ceausescu's rule ended. On October 26, I noted that she did not know the meaning of *glasnost* and *perestroika.* Initially I thought this was a translation problem, but as I probed I saw that she had not previously understood the global reasons for and implications of the rising cost of milk in Romania. Through working with M.B. and her peers, we defined the terms and applied them to Romania and Russia.

Student profile: N.C., female, age 17, grade 12, ethnicity: came from Jamaica seven years ago, activities: track team and church. N.C. is one of the most enthusiastic participants. She read three books during the summer: *Gorky Park, The Three Sisters,* and *The Inspector General.* She also saved newspaper articles. . . . [Yet] initially she did not understand many of the newspaper articles. She was unclear why another man had declared himself president. She did not see the importance of these events to Russia's past, present, and future . . . and was unable to connect the corruption in *Gorky Park* to the corruption that was explained in the newspaper articles. . . . By September 27, she began to ask knowledge-clarification questions in the journal. For example, "Why were the Soviet soldiers in Poland?" I encouraged N.C. to find an answer by giving her clues: "Poland was within the Iron Curtain . . . a satellite of the USSR . . . in the Soviet sphere as a consequence of the Cold War." Although N.C. had completed a United States history course and other social studies courses, she did not recognize these basic terms. I explained the article about Poland in the context of the Cold War, the Iron Curtain, and Soviet satellites.

Student profile: K.F., male, age 17, grade 11, ethnicity: came from Jamaica eight years ago, activities: after-school job, office aide, choir, church. K.F. readily demonstrated his interest and ability to ask analytical questions. After we looked at several magazine articles, he determined that the general theme of almost all news about Russia would fit under the title, "Russia's Road to Democracy." We discussed various aspects of democracy and what democracy was not. After listening to peer talk about the civil war in Azerbaijan, he compared the transition to that of Jamaica.

Student profile: M.M., male, age 16, grade 11, ethnicity: Irish-American, honors classes, activity: swim team. M.M. read Dostoyevsky, Chekhov, and Turgenev during the summer. His father's interest in Marx and political ideologies . . . has helped M.M. gain a broad perspective of different ways of thinking. M.M. articulated his opinion of the meaning of democracy. From the first day, he knew how to formulate questions. For example, he questioned the ability of Russia to develop a democracy with so many different constituencies. . . . About Turgenev's *First Love,* he surmised that Russians have a different attitude toward a woman's taking a leadership role in intimate relationships.

Student profile: L.G., female, age 18, grade 12, ethnicity: Puerto Rican born in New York City, activities: athletics, class officer, civic organizations, numerous clubs. Background: L.G. was discouraged and ready to drop out of the Russian Studies program because she found the summer reading too difficult. She found that she did not understand it. She took part in a summer program at Trinity College that used *The New Yorker* magazine in its curriculum. Her consequent subscription has been her primary source of information about Russia. [During the course of the program] L.G. read Anton Chekhov's, *The Three Sisters.* The following is an excerpt from her report [all sic]:

> In this book I found a lot of sofering. They soffer because they are too educated and find themselves board. They dream of getting out of that town and go to Moscow. . . . The whole story was field with tragedy. Olga, a character in the story, explaining about thre paind she said, "But our sufferings will turn to joy for those on earth, and people living now will be blessed and spoken well of. Dear sisters, our life not ended yet." This means that they have hope for the future.

> Although L.G. found the book difficult, she developed an understanding of what many scholars regard as the essence of the Russian soul: suffering and hope for the future.

Lessons in Providing Equal Access to Knowledge

This second narrative, by Theodore Burkett, comes from his final internship summary. Ted also elected to work at Bulkeley High School in Hartford. Although Ted was preparing to be an English educator, he chose to spend his final or master's year working in a computer writing lab for students with a wide range of special education needs. In his narrative he describes how "equal access" to knowledge, technology, and writing was advanced for the young people he instructed.

A Story of an Inclusive Educator

As the seasons change and the buds blossom, bloom, and grow, I, too, feel the sensation of growth and renewal. Yet I am not a tree that needs the sun, soil, and cloud-brought rain. Rather, I am a teacher stimulated this year by the forces of computers, writing, and some very special students. Over the past year, I have learned a great deal, and in this summary I want to share some of the specific strategies I employed, experiences I enjoyed, and the information I learned.

Coming to Bulkeley at the beginning of the year, I'll now admit, was a bit of a shock. With the imposing and somewhat daunting exterior and the plethora of unsavory stories that abound, . . . I was unsure just what I had gotten myself into. It was going to be a whole year, for better or for worse, and happily I'll say it has definitely been for the better.

My first day of classes was also a bit of a shock. I had not had too much experience with special education students, except for my summer at Windham [his first clinical placement], where I bonded with a twelve-year-old with a disability. Even then, I remarked at how genuine of a soul she had, how easy it was to make her happy. She would clutch my hand each day and run to the swings with me. . . . Little was I to know that the students that I met that first day at Bulkeley would affect me the same way.

At 7:55 that first morning, I had quite the assortment of characters come into the room. Two of these were in wheelchairs, one used his foot to type and drive his wheelchair. Others were of all races and color, sizes, and shapes. . . . After my first day, I questioned what I was doing, but was also excited about teaching this variety of students.

My initial questioning of appearances quickly disappeared as I got to know these students, many of whom were just as wonderful at heart as the twelve-year-old girl I had met two summers ago. But one thing became clear as I began to teach: most of these students had little experience working by themselves. They asked questions even for things that they already knew. I knew that this wouldn't work in my classroom, and instead of giving them answers or doing things for them, I would ask them questions—simple things like what comes at the end of a sentence. . . . Even with spelling, a major problem for my students, my tactic was to not answer them immediately unless the word in question was particularly difficult. I would ask the student, "How do you think you spell it?" About half the time they would know, and they almost always got part of it right. The more often they were right, the less they asked me, and with the aid of the spell check, they were capable of working more and more independently. . . .

One of the goals of the lab was to get them comfortable with the computers and writing on them. By the end of the year, they came in, got their folders, sat down, turned their computers on, and got right to work. They had come a long way since the beginning of the year. . . .

As my students had learned, I also had learned much about teaching strategies, special education, computers, and writing. I feel much more confident and assured dealing with students with dis-abilities. . . . I feel confident with technology, the methodology of teaching using computers, and in my ability to vary strategies for stu-dents of different abilities. . . . I know that this year has better pre-pared me to be a progressive, integrated teacher who is capable of dealing with an extremely diverse student population.

The Teacher-Student Relationship: Learning and Caring

This third account comes from Pamela Pion-Flaherty, also an in-tern at Bulkeley High School, where she had also done her student teaching in special education. Her year was spent coordinating a tu-toring program across subject areas for over 150 students. Her story comes from her acquaintance with a student in one of her special education classes during student teaching, whom she came to know better during her internship year. Pam discusses the effects of caring for a student and how knowing Jack (also known as J.J.) changed her understanding of the relationship between the teacher and her students.

Internship Summary: A Painful Lesson in Teaching

I received a terrific T-shirt for Christmas two years ago. It has a navy blue background. On the front, there is a child reaching up to a bunch of bright stars. The message, for me, conveyed the true meaning of being an educator: "I Touch the Future—I Teach." That was why I wanted to be a teacher. I would take students into my class, teach them, and send them on to the future. I would contribute some insight, some wisdom to their development. I thought of student teaching in terms of how many young people I had reached, had touched in some significant way.

That notion, that understanding of my role as teacher, was challenged—even shattered—on Thursday as I drove home from the funeral of one of my students. Jack was fatally wounded in a drive-by shooting last week. As I drove home, my feelings from throughout the week were intensified. I felt the pain, the anger, the emptiness like never before. A beautiful human being who sat in my class not six months ago was gone forever. My thoughts were no longer of my contributions to his life, but rather of how very much Jack had touched mine. The images of a number of my students came to mind. I thought about how much I had gained from our relationships. I always felt that teaching was rewarding, but now I realize that I had thought that for the wrong reason. I finally can see that while I was busy "making a difference," my students were doing the same.

The experience of the funeral itself was enlightening for me. I saw Jack's family, his brothers and sisters, his parents, aunts, uncles, grandparents, and friends. I thought about how they knew and loved

Jack and how their view likely differed from mine. I tried to imagine Jack in these different roles—son, brother, nephew, and friend. It was a humbling experience for me. While I thought about how well I knew Jack, I knew him only as a student. . . . I was unaware of the other sides of Jack. In fact, no one referred to him as Jack but rather by his nickname, J.J.

While I can't understand or begin to accept the death of such a young person, I can say that I have grown through this experience. I have learned a painful lesson in the reciprocity of the student-teacher relationship. I look toward my future students with a greater love and respect.

An Instance of Stewardship

The last story also takes place in Hartford, but in one of the city's elementary schools. Jennifer Moriarty discusses in her final internship analysis how she learned to be a steward of her school and the school district. She describes her role as the coordinator of two new technology labs in the school and tells of a lab with little or no equipment, of teachers reluctant to use the technology that was available, and of how she convinced the school district to fund a program to help this school.

Learning to Take Initiative

My role as the technology intern at Dwight Elementary School has progressed through many changes over the past school year. When I began my internship, there were no computers available for use and my main responsibility was to prepare for the arrival of the Main Building computers and the construction of the Annex Mac Lab. As the year progressed, so did my role at Dwight. Preparation for the computer labs turned from set-up for the computers into the facilitating of computer use. My role as facilitator continued to grow as the computer lab served increasing numbers of students.

At the start of my internship, the eight IBM-compatible computers had not yet arrived. Further, there was no space available in the Annex to set up the seven Macintosh Classics, which were lent to Dwight by the University of Connecticut. I also found that, due to the rigor of the school day for the staff and administration, there was seldom anyone available for me to ask for instructions pertaining to what needed to be done. The high hopes that I held for my internship were beginning to turn into frustration when I decided that it was time for me to take a step back and reflect upon my situation. At this point, a quotation that Bill Cosby attributed to his father came to mind. At one point, Bill was confused about his situation in life and turned to his father for advice. In reply his father said, "Bill, this is your little red wagon. You can push it, you can pull it, or you can let it stand." Although it is not typical for me to find refuge in quotations, this one proved to be very inspirational to me. It helped me put my situation into perspective: Dwight was my little red wagon and I was going to push it, pull it, or do whatever it took to get my internship under way.

With my change in attitude as ammunition, I began to take initiative in my role as technology intern. I started by acquiring permission to set up the Macintosh computers in the main building . . . and began to develop a small "clientele." It was at this point that I also joined the Technology Task Force and took on numerous responsibilities. . . . Other roles that I took on were making the rounds through the classrooms troubleshooting and facilitating the use of classroom computers, installing software onto the existing computers, and publishing newsletters that kept the staff aware of what was occurring with the development of the labs. Through my own efforts, I became increasingly utilized and I felt more and more positive about my role at Dwight. . . .

[As the year progressed] I collaborated with the Technology Task Force to create a Technology Plan for Dwight. The board of education was offering technology grants, on a competitive basis, to schools that developed the most comprehensive technology plans. When our plan won first place in this competition, which would provide us with thirty computers, thirty printers, and two scanners, we were elated. A matter of weeks later, though, the board of education stated that it was considering rescinding its technology grant, and our elation abruptly ended. In order to voice my opinion, and in the hopes of helping to remedy the situation, I spoke at the next board of education meeting on behalf of Dwight Elementary School and in favor of keeping the grant. I can happily state that the board of education's final decision was to fund the grant as planned.

Upon reflection on my year at Dwight, I view my experience as a great success. I feel that I had many accomplishments that have positively affected both the Dwight community and myself as an individual. . . . I feel that I leave Dwight as a more self-directed and confident person than I was when I went in. Although I had many teachers and students from Dwight thank me for being there to help them out, I tell them, and I know down deep, that they were the ones who helped me.

Ensuring equal access to education for all students may be as much a matter of values as of preparation. Fundamental beliefs and assumptions about persons who appear to be different must shift from fostering segregated service-delivery systems to ensuring equity in education. And given the challenge of educating an increasingly diverse population of students, educators must build new foundations of thinking and practice. We must find for our schools, including postsecondary educational settings, teachers who are willing and able to make appropriate curricular adaptations and who understand the diversity of learners in their classrooms. We need as a society to take seriously the simultaneous renewal of schools and the education of educators.

Education professionals must break barriers between teachers, redesign curricula to allow access to learning for a larger range of students, make strong commitments to preparing teachers differently, and recruit teachers from diverse backgrounds who possess both analytical skills and compassion for people. If the current educational culture, influenced by self-interest and entrenched school organizational structures, has fostered much of what continues to segregate students and isolate them from educational opportunities, then educators must begin to challenge these attitudes and organizations. We all must take bold new looks at the needs of the schools and individuals. We will need to conduct our educational business very differently. We will need to work together. This will be hard work; changing basic beliefs and habits always is. Valuing diversity will not be easy, but it is our moral obligation to try.

Notes

Series Foreword

1. Theodore Roosevelt, "The Manly Virtues and Practical Politics," *Forum* 17 (July 1894): 551.

2. I explored this relationship in *Morality, Efficiency, and Reform: An Interpretation of the History of American Education*, Work in Progress Series no. 5 (Seattle: Institute for Educational Inquiry, 1995).

3. Neil Postman, *The End of Education: Redefining the Value of School* (New York: Vintage, 1996, orig. Knopf, 1995), pp. 5–6.

4. John I. Goodlad, *Educational Renewal: Better Teachers, Better Schools* (San Francisco: Jossey-Bass, 1994), pp. 4–6.

5. John I. Goodlad, *A Place Called School: Prospects for the Future* (New York: McGraw-Hill, 1984); John I. Goodlad, Roger Soder, and Kenneth A. Sirotnik (eds.), *The Moral Dimensions of Teaching* (San Francisco: Jossey-Bass, 1990); John I. Goodlad, Roger Soder, and Kenneth A. Sirotnik (eds.), *Places Where Teachers Are Taught* (San Francisco: Jossey-Bass, 1990); John I. Goodlad, *Teachers for Our Nation's Schools* (San Francisco: Jossey-Bass, 1990); and John I. Goodlad and Pamela Keating (eds.), *Access to Knowledge: An Agenda for Our Nation's Schools* (New York: College Entrance Examination Board, 1990).

By 1997, four more books contributed to the growing literature associated with the Agenda: John I. Goodlad, *Educational Renewal:*

Better Teachers, Better Schools (San Francisco: Jossey-Bass, 1994);
Roger Soder (ed.), *Democracy, Education, and the Schools* (San Francisco: Jossey-Bass, 1996); John I. Goodlad and Timothy J. McMannon (eds.), *The Public Purpose of Education and Schooling* (San Francisco: Jossey-Bass, 1997); and John I. Goodlad, *In Praise of Education* (New York: Teachers College Press, 1997).

6. The postulates were first defined in Goodlad, *Teachers for Our Nation's Schools*, pp. 54–64, and later refined in Goodlad, *Educational Renewal*, pp. 70–94.

Foreword

1. John I. Goodlad, *Teachers for Our Nation's Schools* (San Francisco: Jossey-Bass, 1990).

2. Marvin Wideen, Jolie Mayer-Smith, and Barbara Moon, "A Critical Analysis of the Research on Learning to Teach: Making the Case for an Ecological Perspective on Inquiry," *Review of Educational Research* 68 (Summer 1998): 130–178.

Introduction

1. Kathleen Devaney and Gary Sykes, "Making the Case for Professionalism," in Ann Lieberman (ed.), *Building a Professional Culture in Schools* (New York: Teachers College Press, 1988), p. 4.

2. See John Dewey, *Moral Principles in Education* (Boston: Houghton Mifflin, 1909); John Dewey, *Democracy and Education* (1916; reprint, New York: Free Press, 1966); John I. Goodlad, Roger Soder, and Kenneth A. Sirotnik (eds.), *The Moral Dimensions of Teaching* (San Francisco: Jossey-Bass, 1990); John I. Goodlad, *Teachers for Our Nation's Schools* (San Francisco: Jossey-Bass, 1990); John I. Goodlad, *Educational Renewal: Better Teachers, Better Schools* (San Francisco: Jossey-Bass, 1994); and Hugh Sockett, *The Moral Base for Teacher Professionalism* (New York: Teachers College Press, 1993).

3. John I. Goodlad, "The Occupation of Teaching in Schools," in Goodlad, Soder, and Sirotnik (eds.), *Moral Dimensions of Teaching*, p. 19.

Chapter One

1. Gary D Fenstermacher, "Some Moral Considerations on Teaching as a Profession," in John I. Goodlad, Roger Soder, and Kenneth A. Sirotnik (eds.), *The Moral Dimensions of Teaching* (San Francisco: Jossey-Bass, 1990), p. 148.

2. See Charles W. Case, Judith E. Lanier, and Cecil G. Miskel, "The Holmes Group Report: Impetus for Gaining Professional Status for Teachers," *Journal of Teacher Education* 37 (July–August 1986): 36–43; William J. Goode, "The Librarian: From Occupation to Profession?" *Library Quarterly* 31 (October 1961): 306–320; Ernest Greenwood, "Attributes of a Profession," *Social Work* 2 (July 1957): 45–55; Wilbert E. Moore, *The Professions: Roles and Rules* (New York: Russell Sage Foundation, 1970); and Howard M. Vollmer and Donald L. Mills (eds.), *Professionalization* (Englewood Cliffs, N.J.: Prentice-Hall, 1966).

3. See Paul Starr, *The Social Transformation of American Medicine* (New York: Basic Books, 1982); Robert Stevens, *Law School: Legal Education in America from the 1850s to the 1980s* (Chapel Hill: University of North Carolina Press, 1983); William M. Sullivan, *Work and Integrity: The Crisis and Promise of Professionalism in America* (New York: HarperCollins, 1995); and Harold L. Wilensky, "The Professionalization of Everyone?" *American Journal of Sociology* 70 (September 1964): 137–158.

4. Many excellent sources detail and analyze the history of schooling, teaching, and teacher education. See, among others, Landon E. Beyer and others, *Preparing Teachers as Professionals: The Role of Educational Studies and Other Liberal Disciplines* (New York: Teachers College Press, 1989); James Bryant Conant, *The Education of American Teachers* (New York: McGraw-Hill, 1963); Lawrence A. Cremin, "The Heritage of American Teacher Education," part I, *Journal of Teacher Education* 4 (June 1953): 163–170, and part II, *Journal of Teacher Education* 4 (September 1953): 246–250; Jurgen Herbst, *And Sadly Teach: Teacher Education and Professionalization in American Culture* (Madison: University of Wisconsin Press, 1989); Dan C. Lortie, *Schoolteacher: A Sociological Study* (Chicago:

University of Chicago Press, 1975); Timothy J. McMannon, *Morality, Efficiency, and Reform: An Interpretation of the History of American Education*, Work in Progress Series no. 5 (Seattle: Institute for Educational Inquiry, 1995); and David B. Tyack, *The One Best System: A History of American Education* (Cambridge, Mass.: Harvard University Press, 1974).

5. Sullivan, *Work and Integrity*, p. 2.

6. Hugh Sockett, *The Moral Base for Teacher Professionalism* (New York: Teachers College Press, 1993), p. 108.

7. Amitai Etzioni, *The Semi-Professions and Their Organization: Teachers, Nurses, Social Workers* (New York: Free Press, 1969).

8. Sullivan, *Work and Integrity*, pp. 147–148.

9. Anthony Jones (ed.), *Professions and the State: Expertise and Autonomy in the Soviet Union and Eastern Europe* (Philadelphia: Temple University Press, 1991), pp. vii–x.

10. Konrad H. Jarausch, *The Unfree Professions: German Lawyers, Teachers, and Engineers, 1900–1950* (New York: Oxford University Press, 1990), p. vii.

11. Jarausch, *Unfree Professions*, p. 209.

12. Jarausch, *Unfree Professions*, p. 227.

13. Jones (ed.), *Professions and the State*, p. ix.

14. Elliott A. Krause, "Professions and the State in the Soviet Union and Eastern Europe: Theoretical Issues," in Jones (ed.), *Professions and the State*, pp. 35–36.

15. Sullivan, *Work and Integrity*, p. 28.

16. John I. Goodlad, "The Occupation of Teaching in Schools," in Goodlad, Soder, and Sirotnik (eds.), *Moral Dimensions of Teaching*, p. 27.

17. Vivian Fueyo and Mark Koorland, "Teacher As Researcher: A Synonym for Professionalism," *Journal of Teacher Education* 48 (November–December 1997): 336.

18. Sockett, *Moral Base for Teacher Professionalism*, p. 129.

19. Sullivan, *Work and Integrity*, p. 187.

20. Andy Hargreaves and Ivor Goodson, "Teachers' Professional Lives: Aspirations and Actualities," in Ivor F. Goodson and Andy Hargreaves (eds.), *Teachers' Professional Lives* (London: Falmer, 1996), p. 13.

21. Sullivan, *Work and Integrity*, p. 195.

22. Goodlad, "The Occupation of Teaching in Schools," p. 6.

23. Goodlad, "The Occupation of Teaching in Schools," p. 29.

24. Roger Soder, "The Rhetoric of Teacher Professionalization," in Goodlad, Soder, and Sirotnik (eds.), *Moral Dimensions of Teaching*, pp. 72–73.

25. Fenstermacher, "Some Moral Considerations on Teaching as a Profession," pp. 132–133.

26. John Dewey, *Moral Principles in Education* (Boston: Houghton Mifflin, 1909), pp. 57–58.

27. See, for example, Goodlad, Soder, and Sirotnik (eds.), *Moral Dimensions of Teaching*.

28. John I. Goodlad, *Educational Renewal: Better Teachers, Better Schools* (San Francisco: Jossey-Bass, 1994), p. 43.

29. R. S. Peters, *Ethics and Education* (Glenview, Ill.: Scott, Foresman, 1967), p. 23.

30. Michael Eraut, *Developing Professional Knowledge and Competence* (London: Falmer, 1994), p. 68.

31. For a detailed discussion of these four moral dimensions of teaching, see John I. Goodlad, *Teachers for Our Nation's Schools* (San Francisco: Jossey-Bass, 1990), pp. 46–53.

32. Goodlad, "The Occupation of Teaching in Schools," p. 19.

33. Sockett, *Moral Base for Teacher Professionalism*, pp. 1–17.

34. Sockett, *Moral Base for Teacher Professionalism*, p. 16.

35. Landon E. Beyer, "The Moral Contours of Teacher Education," *Journal of Teacher Education* 48 (September–October 1997): 246–247.

36. Sockett, *Moral Base for Teacher Professionalism*, p. 9.

37. Stephen Edelston Toulmin, *An Examination of the Place of Reason in Ethics* (Cambridge, England: Cambridge University Press, 1950), p. 1.

38. National Education Association, "Code of Ethics of the Education Profession." Available at http://www.nea.org/info/code.html. Accessed February 5, 1999.

39. National Education Association, "Code of Ethics," pp. 1–2.

40. John W. Brubacher, Charles W. Case, and Timothy G. Reagan, *Becoming a Reflective Educator: How to Build a Culture of Inquiry in the Schools* (Thousand Oaks, Calif.: Corwin, 1994), pp. 120–121.

41. John Dewey, *The Public and Its Problems* (New York: Henry Holt, 1927), pp. 208–209.

Chapter Two

1. John Dewey, *How We Think* (Boston: Heath, 1910), p. 13.

2. See B. Paul Komisar and James E. McClellan, "The Logic of Slogans," in B. Othanel Smith and Robert H. Ennis (eds.), *Language and Concepts in Education* (Chicago: Rand McNally, 1961), pp. 195–214.

3. Robert Fitzgibbons, *Making Educational Decisions: An Introduction to Philosophy of Education* (New York: Harcourt Brace Jovanovich, 1981), pp. 13–14.

4. Quoted in Judith Irwin, "What Is a Reflective/Analytical Teacher?" (Storrs: School of Education, University of Connecticut, 1987, photocopy), p. 1.

5. Cornel M. Hamm, *Philosophical Issues in Education: An Introduction* (New York: Falmer, 1989), p. 163.

6. Student interview, May 1994.

7. Charles E. Silberman, *Crisis in the Classroom: The Remaking of American Education* (New York: Random House, 1971), p. 380.

8. Mark Van Doren, *Liberal Education* (Boston: Beacon Press, 1959), pp. 170–171.

9. Thomas F. Green, "The Formation of Conscience in an Age of Technology," *American Journal of Education* 94 (November 1985): 4.

10. Donald A. Schön, *The Reflective Practitioner: How Professionals Think in Action* (New York: Basic Books, 1983), and *Educating the Reflective Practitioner: Toward a New Design for Teaching and Learning in the Professions* (San Francisco: Jossey-Bass, 1987).

11. Catherine Fosnot, *Enquiring Teachers, Enquiring Learners: A Constructivist Approach to Teaching* (New York: Teachers College Press, 1989), p. xi.

12. Joellen P. Killion and Guy R. Todnem, "A Process for Personal Theory Building," *Educational Leadership* 48 (March 1991): 15.

13. Killion and Todnem, "Process for Personal Theory Building," p. 15.

14. Max van Manen, "Linking Ways of Knowing with Ways of Being Practical," *Curriculum Inquiry* 6 (1977): 226–227.

15. Irwin, "What Is a Reflective/Analytical Teacher?" p. 5.

16. Daniel Broderick III, "Internship Summary" (student paper, School of Education, University of Connecticut, Storrs, May 1994).

17. Brian Keating, "Internship Summary" (student paper, School of Education, University of Connecticut, Storrs, December 1993).

18. Georgea Mohlman Sparks-Langer and Amy Berstein Colton, "Synthesis of Research on Teachers' Reflective Thinking," *Educational Leadership* 48 (March 1991): 37–44.

19. Lee S. Shulman, "Knowledge and Teaching: Foundations of the New Reform," *Harvard Educational Review* 57 (February 1987): 8.

20. See David C. Berliner, "In Pursuit of the Expert Pedagogue," *Educational Researcher* 15 (August–September 1986): 5–13; and Sparks-Langer and Colton, "Teachers' Reflective Thinking," pp. 37–38.

21. Berliner, "Expert Pedagogue," p. 10.

22. Sparks-Langer and Colton, "Teachers' Reflective Thinking," p. 38.

23. Sparks-Langer and Colton, "Teachers' Reflective Thinking," p. 39.

24. See Stanton M. Teal and Gerald M. Reagan, "Educational Goals," in Jack R. Frymier (ed.), *A School for Tomorrow* (Berkeley: McCutchan, 1973), pp. 37–84.

25. Sparks-Langer and Colton, "Teachers' Reflective Thinking," p. 41.

26. See F. Michael Connelly and D. Jean Clandinin, "Stories of Experience and Narrative Inquiry," *Educational Researcher* 19 (June–July 1990): 2–14; Dixie Goswami and Peter R. Stillman (eds.), *Reclaiming the Classroom: Teacher Research as an Agency for Change* (Upper Montclair, N.J.: Boynton/Cook, 1987); and Kenneth M. Zeichner and Daniel P. Liston, "Teaching Student Teachers to Reflect," *Harvard Educational Review* 57 (February 1987): 23–48.

27. Student interview, May 1994.

28. See, for example, John W. Brubacher, Charles W. Case, and Timothy G. Reagan, *Becoming a Reflective Educator: How to Build a Culture of Inquiry in the Schools* (Thousand Oaks, Calif.: Corwin, 1994); Irwin, "What Is a Reflective/Analytical Teacher?"; Timothy G. Reagan, "Educating the 'Reflective Practitioner': The Contribution of Philosophy of Education," *Journal of Research and Development in Education* 26 (Summer 1993): 189–196; Timothy G. Reagan and others, "Reflecting on 'Reflective Practice': Implications for Teacher Evaluation," *Journal of Personnel Evaluation in Education* 6 (February 1992): 263–277; and Timothy G. Reagan, Charles W. Case, and Kay A. Norlander, "Toward Reflective Teacher Education: The University of Connecticut Experience," *International Journal of Educational Reform* 2 (October 1993): 399–406.

29. Irwin, "What Is a Reflective/Analytical Teacher?" p. 6.

30. Charles W. Case, Judith E. Lanier, and Cecil G. Miskel, "The Holmes Group Report: Impetus for Gaining Professional Status for Teachers," *Journal of Teacher Education* 37 (July–August 1986): 36.

31. D. C. Phillips, *Philosophy, Science, and Social Inquiry: Contemporary Methodological Controversies in Social Science and Related Applied Fields of Research* (Oxford: Pergamon Press, 1987), p. vii.

32. See Goswami and Stillman, *Reclaiming the Classroom*.

33. Dorene D. Ross, Elizabeth Bondy, and Diane W. Kyle, *Reflective Teaching for Student Empowerment: Elementary Curriculum and Methods* (New York: Macmillan, 1993), p. 337.

34. Teacher interview, June 1994.

35. James McKernan, *Curriculum Action Research: A Handbook of Methods and Resources for the Reflective Practitioner* (New York: St. Martin's Press, 1991), p. ix.

36. Elliott W. Eisner and Alan Peshkin (eds.), *Qualitative Inquiry in Education: The Continuing Debate* (New York: Teachers College Press, 1990), p. 3.

37. See Robert C. Bogdan and Sari K. Biklen, *Qualitative Research for Education: An Introduction to Theory and Methods*, 3rd ed. (Needham Heights, Mass.: Allyn and Bacon, 1998); Corinne E. Glesne and Alan Peshkin, *Becoming Qualitative Researchers: An Introduction* (White Plains, N.Y.: Longman, 1992); Yvonna S. Lincoln and Egon G. Guba, *Naturalistic Inquiry* (Beverly Hills, Calif.: Sage, 1985); Alan Peshkin, "The Goodness of Qualitative Research," *Educational Researcher* 22 (March 1993): 23–29; Suzanne M. Wilson, "Not Tension But Intention: A Response to Wong's Analysis of the Researcher/Teacher," *Educational Researcher* 24 (November 1995): 19–22; E. David Wong, "Challenges Confronting the Researcher/Teacher: Conflicts of Purpose and Conduct," *Educational Researcher* 24 (April 1995): 22–28; and E. David Wong, "Challenges Confronting the Researcher/Teacher: A Rejoinder to Wilson," *Educational Researcher* 24 (November 1995): 22–23.

38. Bogdan and Biklen, *Qualitative Research for Education*, p. 230.

39. See Brubacher, Case, and Reagan, *Becoming a Reflective Educator*; Renee T. Clift, W. Robert Houston, and Marleen C. Pugach (eds.), *Encouraging Reflective Practice in Education: An Analysis of Issues and Programs* (New York: Teachers College Press, 1990); Marilyn Cochran-Smith and Susan L. Lytle, "Research on Teaching and Teacher Research: The Issues That Divide," *Educational Researcher* 19 (March 1990): 2–10; Marilyn Cochran-Smith and Susan L. Lytle (eds.), *Inside/Outside: Teacher Research and Knowledge* (New York: Teachers College Press, 1993; Susan L. Lytle and Marilyn Cochran-Smith, "Teacher Research as a Way of Knowing," *Harvard Educational Review* 62 (Winter 1992): 447–474.

40. Lytle and Cochran-Smith, "Teacher Research as a Way of Knowing," p. 470.

41. See Stephen Kemmis and Robin McTaggart (eds.), *The Action Research Planner*, 3rd ed. (Victoria, Australia: Deakin University Press, 1988).

42. Kenneth A. Sirotnik, "The Meaning and Conduct of Inquiry in School-University Partnerships," in Kenneth A. Sirotnik and John I. Goodlad (eds.), *School-University Partnerships in Action: Concepts, Cases, and Concerns* (New York: Teachers College Press, 1988), p. 187.

43. John W. Best and James V. Kahn, *Research in Education*, 8th ed. (Boston: Allyn & Bacon, 1998), p. 21.

44. Michael Quinn Patton, *Qualitative Evaluation and Research Methods*, 2nd ed. (Newbury Park, Calif.: Sage, 1990), p. 157.

45. Patricia Clifford and Sharon L. Friesen, "A Curious Plan: Managing on the Twelfth," *Harvard Educational Review* 63 (Fall 1993): 356–357.

46. See, however, Reagan and others, "Reflecting on 'Reflective Practice.'"

47. Dorene D. Ross, "Programmatic Structures for the Preparation of Reflective Teachers," in Clift, Houston, and Pugach (eds.), *Encouraging Reflective Practice in Education*, p. 113.

48. Kenneth A. Sirotnik, "Evaluation in the Ecology of Schooling: The Process of School Renewal," in John I. Goodlad (ed.), *The Ecology of School Renewal: Eighty-Sixth Yearbook of the National Society for the Study of Education* (Chicago: National Society for the Study of Education, 1987), p. 51.

49. Joint Committee on Standards for Educational Evaluation, *The Personnel Evaluation Standards: How to Assess Systems for Evaluating Educators* (Newbury Park, Calif.: Sage, 1988), p. 5.

50. Susan M. Johnson, *Teachers at Work: Achieving Success in Our Schools* (New York: Basic, 1990).

51. Quoted in Johnson, *Teachers at Work*, p. 269.

52. Quoted in Johnson, *Teachers at Work*, p. 274.

53. See James S. Cangelosi, *Evaluating Classroom Instruction* (New York: Longman, 1991); and Johnson, *Teachers at Work*.

54. Johnson, *Teachers at Work*, p. 276.

55. Cangelosi, *Evaluating Classroom Instruction*.

56. Thomas L. Good and Catherine Mulryan, "Teacher Ratings: A Call for Teacher Control and Self-Evaluation," in Jason Millman and Linda Darling-Hammond (eds.), *The New Handbook of Teacher Evaluation: Assessing Elementary and Secondary School Teachers* (Newbury Park, Calif.: Sage, 1990), p. 201.

57. See, for example, Good and Mulryan, "Teacher Ratings."

58. Edward F. Iwanicki, "Teacher Evaluation for School Improvement," in Millman and Darling-Hammond (eds.), *New Handbook of Teacher Evaluation*, p. 159.

59. Iwanicki, "Teacher Evaluation for School Improvement."

60. Milbrey Wallin McLaughlin and R. Scott Pfeifer, *Teacher Evaluation: Improvement, Accountability, and Effective Learning* (New York: Teachers College Press, 1988), p. 85.

61. McLaughlin and Pfeifer, *Teacher Evaluation*, p. 87.

62. See David M. Fetterman (ed.), *Ethnography in Educational Evaluation* (Beverly Hills, Calif.: Sage, 1984); and Patton, *Qualitative Evaluation and Research Methods*.

63. See Shulman, "Knowledge and Teaching."

Chapter Three

1. David P. Page, *Theory and Practice of Teaching: Or, The Motives and Methods of Good School-Keeping* (Syracuse: Hall & Dickson, 1847), pp. 9–10.

2. John Dewey, *Democracy and Education* (1916; reprint, New York: Free Press, 1966), p. 107.

3. See John I. Goodlad, *Educational Renewal: Better Teachers, Better Schools* (San Francisco: Jossey-Bass, 1994), on "simultaneous renewal."

4. See Charles W. Case, Judith E. Lanier, and Cecil G. Miskel, "The Holmes Group Report: Impetus for Gaining Professional Status for Teachers," *Journal of Teacher Education* 37 (July–August 1986): 36–43.

5. See John I. Goodlad, "The Occupation of Teaching in Schools," in John I. Goodlad, Roger Soder, and Kenneth A. Sirotnik (eds.), *The Moral Dimensions of Teaching* (San Francisco: Jossey-Bass, 1990), pp. 20–27; John I. Goodlad, *Teachers for Our Nation's Schools* (San Francisco: Jossey-Bass, 1990), p. 52; John I. Goodlad, "The Moral Dimensions of Schooling and Teacher Education," *Journal of Moral Education* 21:2 (1992): 87–97; and Goodlad, *Educational Renewal*, pp. 4–5.

6. Goodlad, *Teachers for Our Nation's Schools*, p. 59.

7. John Dewey, *Moral Principles in Education* (Boston: Houghton Mifflin, 1909), p. 58.

8. Goodlad, *Educational Renewal*, p. 4.

9. Dewey, *Democracy and Education*, p. 87.

10. Robert B. Westbrook, "Public Schooling and American Democracy," in Roger Soder (ed.), *Democracy, Education, and the Schools* (San Francisco: Jossey-Bass, 1996), p. 145. The Walzer quotation is from "Citizenship," in Terence Ball, James Farr, and Russell L. Hanson (eds.), *Political Innovation and Conceptual Change* (Cambridge, England: Cambridge University Press, 1989), p. 218.

11. Martin Semmel, journal entry (student paper, School of Education, University of Connecticut, Storrs, February 15, 1996).

12. Jonathan Kozol, *Savage Inequalities: Children in America's Schools* (New York: Crown, 1991), pp. 51–52.

13. John I. Goodlad, "Access to Knowledge," in John I. Goodlad and Thomas C. Lovitt (eds.), *Integrating General and Special Education* (New York: Macmillan, 1993), p. 2.

14. Future social studies/history teacher, "Statement of Philosophy in Exceptionality I" (student paper, School of Education, University of Connecticut, Storrs, December 1995).

15. Future elementary educator, "Statement of Philosophy in Exceptionality I" (student paper, School of Education, University of Connecticut, Storrs, December 1995).

16. Donna H. Kerr, *Beyond Education: In Search of Nurture*, Work in Progress Series no. 2 (Seattle: Institute for Educational Inquiry, 1993), p. 10.

17. Goodlad, *Teachers for Our Nation's Schools*, p. 49.

18. Dewey, *Democracy and Education*, p. 160.

19. Theodore J. Kopcha, "Final Internship Summary" (student paper, School of Education, University of Connecticut, Storrs, May 1996).

20. Semmel, journal entry, March 5, 1996.

21. Jennifer A. Del Conte, journal entry (student paper, School of Education, University of Connecticut, Storrs, December 1995).

22. Jennifer A. Del Conte, personal communication with author, March 13, 1996.

23. Goodlad, *Teachers for Our Nation's Schools*, pp. 43–44.

24. Goodlad, *Teachers for Our Nation's Schools*, p. 44.

25. Student interview, May 1995.

26. Kopcha, "Final Internship Summary."

27. Goodlad, *Teachers for Our Nation's Schools*, p. 242.

28. Ernest L. Boyer, *Scholarship Reconsidered: Priorities of the Professoriate* (Princeton, N.J.: Carnegie Foundation for the Advancement of Teaching, 1990).

29. See Goodlad, *Teachers for Our Nation's Schools*, chaps. 8, 9; Goodlad, *Educational Renewal*; and Roger Soder, "American Education: Facing up to Unspoken Assumptions," *Daedalus* 124 (Fall 1995): 163–167.

30. Goodlad, *Educational Renewal*, pp. 19–20.

31. See Case, Lanier, and Miskel, "The Holmes Group Report"; and Kenneth A. Strike, "Is Teaching a Profession: How Would We Know?" *Journal of Personnel Evaluation in Education* 4 (September 1990): 91–117.

32. See Timothy G. Reagan, Charles W. Case, and Kay A. Norlander, "Toward Reflective Teacher Education: The University of Connecticut Experience," *International Journal of Education Reform* 2 (October 1993): 399–406.

33. See Kay A. Norlander, Charles W. Case, Timothy G. Reagan, and Pamela Campbell, "The Role of Collaborative Inquiry and Reflective Practice in Teacher Preparation and the Reform of American

Education" (paper presented at the annual meeting of the American Association of Colleges for Teacher Education, Phoenix, February 1997).

34. See Hendrik D. Gideonse, "Organizing Schools to Encourage Teacher Inquiry," in Richard F. Elmore and others (eds.), *Restructuring Schools: The Next Generation of Educational Reform* (San Francisco: Jossey-Bass, 1990), pp. 97–124; and Kenneth A. Sirotnik, "The Meaning and Conduct of Inquiry in School-University Partnerships," in Kenneth A. Sirotnik and John I. Goodlad (eds.), *School-University Partnerships in Action: Concepts, Cases, and Concerns* (New York: Teachers College Press, 1988), pp. 169–190.

35. Goodlad, *Educational Renewal*, p. 271.

36. John Dewey, *How We Think: A Restatement of the Relation of Reflective Thinking to the Educative Process*, rev. ed. (Boston: D. C. Heath, 1933); Concha Delgado-Gaitan, "Researching Change and Changing the Researcher," *Harvard Educational Review* 63 (Winter 1993): 389–411; Barre Toelken, "Fieldwork Enlightenment," *Parabola* 20 (Summer 1995): 28–35; Mary Catherine Bateson, *Peripheral Visions: Learning Along the Way* (New York: HarperCollins, 1994); Margery Wolf, *A Thrice-Told Tale: Feminism, Postmodernism, and Ethnographic Responsibility* (Stanford: Stanford University Press, 1992); Marilyn Cochran-Smith and Susan L. Lytle (eds.), *Inside/Outside: Teacher Research and Knowledge* (New York: Teachers College Press, 1993); and Mary Field Belenky, Blythe McVicker Clinchy, Nancy Rule Goldberger, and Jill Mattuck Tarule, *Women's Ways of Knowing: The Development of Self, Voice, and Mind* (New York: Basic Books, 1986).

37. Roger Soder, "Teaching in a Democracy: The Role of the Arts and Sciences in the Preparation of Teachers," Occasional Paper no. 19 (Seattle: Center for Educational Renewal, University of Washington, June 1994), pp. 16–17.

38. See, among others, James Bryant Conant, *The Education of American Teachers* (New York: McGraw-Hill, 1963); James O. Freedman, *Idealism and Liberal Education* (Ann Arbor: University of Michigan Press, 1996); Goodlad, *Educational Renewal*; and Holmes Group, *Tomorrow's Teachers: A Report of the Holmes Group* (East Lansing, Mich.: Holmes Group, 1986).

39. Freedman, *Idealism and Liberal Education*, p. 1.

40. Freedman, *Idealism and Liberal Education*, p. 2.

41. Soder, "Teaching in a Democracy," p. 4.

42. Hugh Sockett, *The Moral Base for Teacher Professionalism* (New York: Teachers College Press, 1993), p. 7.

43. Nel Noddings, *The Challenge to Care in Schools: An Alternative Approach to Education* (New York: Teachers College Press, 1992), pp. 177–178.

44. Noddings, *Challenge to Care in Schools*, p. 178.

45. Holmes Group, *Tomorrow's Teachers*.

46. Noddings, *Challenge to Care in Schools*, p. 179.

47. In addition to Goodlad's *Teachers for Our Nation's Schools* and *Educational Renewal*, see Robert S. Patterson, Nicholas M. Michelli, and Arturo Pacheco, *Centers of Pedagogy: New Structures for Educational Renewal* (San Francisco: Jossey-Bass, 1999).

48. Lorianne Brown, internship description (student paper, School of Education, University of Connecticut, Storrs, May 1996).

49. Goodlad, *Educational Renewal*, p. 46.

50. Ruth W. Grant, "The Ethics of Talk: Classroom Conversation and Democratic Politics," *Teachers College Record* 97 (Spring 1996): 474–475.

51. Grant, "Ethics of Talk," p. 477.

52. Ira Shor and Paulo Freire, *A Pedagogy for Liberation: Dialogues on Transforming Education* (South Hadley, Mass.: Bergin & Garvey, 1987), p. 13.

53. Del Conte, journal entry, December 1995.

54. John Angus Campbell, "Oratory, Democracy, and the Classroom," in Soder (ed.), *Democracy, Education, and the Schools*, p. 217.

55. Martin Semmel, "Internship Summary" (student paper, School of Education, University of Connecticut, Storrs, May 1996).

56. Christopher Islaub, "Final Internship Summary: The Year in Review" (student paper, School of Education, University of Connecticut, Storrs, May 1997).

Chapter Four

1. See Robert N. Bellah and others, *Habits of the Heart: Individualism and Commitment in American Life* (Berkeley: University of California Press, 1985); Robert N. Bellah and others, *The Good Society* (New York: Knopf, 1991); Amitai Etzioni, *The Spirit of Community: Rights, Responsibilities, and the Communitarian Agenda* (New York: Crown, 1993); Gary D Fenstermacher, "On Restoring Public and Private Life," in John I. Goodlad and Timothy J. McMannon (eds.), *The Public Purpose of Education and Schooling* (San Francisco: Jossey-Bass, 1997), pp. 55–71; and John I. Goodlad, "Democracy, Education, and Community," in Roger Soder (ed.), *Democracy, Education, and the Schools* (San Francisco: Jossey-Bass, 1996), pp. 87–124.

2. Plato, *The Republic*, trans. Allan Bloom (New York: Basic Books, 1968), p. 198.

3. John Dewey, *The School and Society* (Chicago: University of Chicago Press, 1900), p. 7.

4. John I. Goodlad, *Educational Renewal: Better Teachers, Better Schools* (San Francisco: Jossey-Bass, 1994), p. 224.

5. Ernest L. Boyer, *The Basic School: A Community for Learning* (Princeton, N.J.: Carnegie Foundation for the Advancement of Teaching, 1995), p. 17.

6. Daniel Perlstein, "Community and Democracy in American Schools: Arthurdale and the Fate of Progressive Education," *Teachers College Record* 97 (Summer 1996): 646.

7. John I. Goodlad, *Teachers for Our Nation's Schools* (San Francisco: Jossey-Bass, 1990), p. 288.

8. Sandra R. Schecter and Shawn Parkhurst, "Ideological Differences in a Teacher-Research Group," *American Educational Research Journal* 30 (Winter 1993): 794.

9. Interview of future elementary educator, May 1994.

10. Kerri Kearney, "Description of Internship" (student paper, School of Education, University of Connecticut, Storrs, December 1995).

11. Heather Mikaitis, "Internship Summary" (student paper, School of Education, University of Connecticut, Storrs, May 1995).

12. Brian Keating, "Internship Summary" (student paper, School of Education, University of Connecticut, Storrs, December 1993).

13. Richard Abrams, "Internship Summary" (student paper, School of Education, University of Connecticut, Storrs, May 1994).

14. See Magnus O. Bassey, "Teachers as Cultural Brokers in the Midst of Diversity," *Educational Foundations* 10 (Spring 1996): 37–52; Maurice Craft, "Cultural Diversity and Teacher Education," in Maurice Craft (ed.), *Teacher Education in Plural Societies: An International Review* (London: Falmer, 1996), pp. 1–15; Henry A. Giroux, *Border Crossings: Cultural Workers and the Politics of Education* (New York: Routledge, 1992); Jonathan Kozol, *Savage Inequalities: Children in America's Schools* (New York: Crown, 1991); Sharon Quint, *Schooling Homeless Children: A Working Model for America's Public Schools* (New York: Teachers College Press, 1994); and Ira Shor and Paulo Freire, *A Pedagogy for Liberation: Dialogues on Transforming Education* (South Hadley, Mass.: Bergin & Garvey, 1987).

15. John I. Goodlad, "Toward a Healthy Ecosystem," in John I. Goodlad (ed.), *The Ecology of School Renewal: Eighty-Sixth Yearbook of the National Society for the Study of Education* (Chicago: National Society for the Study of Education, 1987), p. 218.

16. Paulo Freire in Shor and Freire, *Pedagogy for Liberation*, p. 181.

17. See, among others, Kozol, *Savage Inequalities*; and David B. Tyack, *The One Best System: A History of American Urban Education* (Cambridge, Mass.: Harvard University Press, 1974).

18. C. A. Bowers and David J. Flinders, *Responsive Teaching: An Ecological Approach to Classroom Patterns of Language, Culture, and Thought* (New York: Teachers College Press, 1990); Kris D. Gutierrez and Brenda Meyer, "Creating Communities of Effective Practice: Building Literacy for Language Minority Students," in Jeannie Oakes and Karen Hunter Quartz (eds.), *Creating New Educational Communities: Ninety-Fourth Yearbook of the National Society for the Study of Education*, part I (Chicago: National Society for the Study of Education, 1995), pp. 32–52; and Paul Heckman, "Understanding School Culture," in Goodlad (ed.), *Ecology of School Renewal*, pp. 63–78.

19. See Goodlad, "Toward a Healthy Ecosystem"; John I. Goodlad,

Toward Educative Communities and Tomorrow's Teachers, Work in Progress Series no. 1 (Seattle: Institute for Educational Inquiry, 1992); Goodlad, *Educational Renewal*; Oakes and Quartz (eds.), *Creating New Educational Communities*; and Marleen C. Pugach and Barbara L. Seidl, "From Exclusion to Inclusion in Urban Schools: A New Case for Teacher Education Reform," *Education and Urban Society* 27 (August 1995): 379–395.

20. In Shor and Freire, *Pedagogy for Liberation*, p. 181.

21. See John I. Goodlad, "Access to Knowledge," in John I. Goodlad and Thomas C. Lovitt (eds.), *Integrating General and Special Education* (New York: Macmillan, 1993), pp. 1–22; John I. Goodlad, "Common Schools for the Common Weal: Reconciling Self-Interest with the Common Good," in John I. Goodlad and Pamela Keating (eds.), *Access to Knowledge: The Continuing Agenda for Our Nation's Schools*, rev. ed. (New York: College Entrance Examination Board, 1994), pp. 1–21; and John I. Goodlad, Roger Soder, and Kenneth A. Sirotnik (eds.), *The Moral Dimensions of Teaching* (San Francisco: Jossey-Bass, 1990).

22. Bowers and Flinders, *Responsive Teaching*, pp. 225–226.

23. Lorianne Brown, "Internship Summary" (student paper, School of Education, University of Connecticut, Storrs, October 1995).

24. Donnah Rochester, "Internship Summary" (student paper, School of Education, University of Connecticut, Storrs, May 1994).

25. Jonathan Jette, "Internship Summary" (student paper, School of Education, University of Connecticut, Storrs, May 1995).

26. Roy J. Creek, "The Professional Development School: Tomorrow's School or Today's Fantasy," in Hugh G. Petrie (ed.), *Professionalization, Partnership, and Power: Building Professional Development Schools* (Albany: State University of New York Press, 1995), p. 250.

27. See, for example, Charles W. Case, Kay A. Norlander, and Timothy G. Reagan, "Cultural Transformation in an Urban Professional Development Center: Policy Implications for School-University Collaboration," *Educational Policy* 7 (March 1993): 40–60; Linda Darling-Hammond, *Professional Development Schools: Schools for De-*

veloping a Profession (New York: Teachers College Press, 1994); Michael Fullan, *Change Forces: Probing the Depths of Educational Reform* (New York: Falmer, 1993); Holmes Group, *Tomorrow's Teachers: A Report of the Holmes Group* (East Lansing, Mich.: Holmes Group, 1986); Holmes Group, *Tomorrow's Schools: Principles for the Design of Professional Development Schools* (East Lansing, Mich.: Holmes Group, 1990); Holmes Group, *Tomorrow's Schools of Education: A Report of the Holmes Group* (East Lansing, Mich.: Holmes Group, 1996); Marsha Levine, "A Conceptual Framework for Professional Practice Schools," in Marsha Levine (ed.), *Professional Practice Schools: Linking Teacher Education and School Reform* (New York: Teachers College Press, 1992), pp. 8–24; Pugach and Seidl, "From Exclusion to Inclusion in Urban Schools"; Judith Haymore Sandholtz and Ellen C. Finan, "Blurring the Boundaries to Promote School-University Partnerships," *Journal of Teacher Education* 49 (January–February 1998): 13–25; Kenneth A. Sirotnik, "The Meaning and Conduct of Inquiry in School-University Partnerships," in Kenneth A. Sirotnik and John I. Goodlad (eds.), *School-University Partnerships in Action: Concepts, Cases, and Concerns* (New York: Teachers College Press, 1988), pp. 169–190; and Trish Stoddart, "The Professional Development School: Building Bridges Between Cultures," in Petrie (ed.), *Professionalization, Partnership, and Power*, pp. 41–59.

28. Case, Norlander, and Reagan, "Cultural Transformation in an Urban Professional Development Center"; Creek, "The Professional Development School"; Goodlad, *Teachers for Our Nation's Schools*; and Lee Teitel, "Can School-University Partnerships Lead to the Simultaneous Renewal of Schools and Teacher Education?" *Journal of Teacher Education* 45 (September–October 1994): 245–252, among others.

29. Francis Fukuyama, *Trust: The Social Virtues and the Creation of Prosperity* (New York: Free Press, 1995); Jennifer Nias, "The Nature of Trust," in John Elliott and others (eds.), *School Accountability* (London: Grant McIntyre, 1975); Robert D. Putnam with Robert Leonardi and Raffaella Y. Nanetti, *Making Democracy Work: Civic Traditions in Modern Italy* (Princeton, N.J.: Princeton University

Press, 1993); Hugh Sockett, *The Moral Base for Teacher Professionalism* (New York: Teachers College Press, 1993); and Patricia White, *Civic Virtues and Public Schooling: Educating Citizens for a Democratic Society* (New York: Teachers College Press, 1996).

30. Janet Benton and others, "Negotiating School-University Partnerships: Participants' Voices in Co-Reform," *Urban Review* 28 (September 1996); Robert V. Bullough, Jr., and others, "Long-Term PDS Development in Research Universities and the Clinicalization of Teacher Education," *Journal of Teacher Education* 48 (March–April 1997): 85–95; Case, Norlander, and Reagan, "Cultural Transformation in an Urban Professional Development Center"; Michelle Collay, "Creating a Common Ground: The Facilitator's Role in Initiating School-University Partnerships," in Petrie (ed.), *Professionalization, Partnership, and Power*, pp. 145–157; and Stoddart, "The Professional Development School."

31. Putnam, *Making Democracy Work*; and Scott R. Sweetland, "Human Capital Theory: Foundations of a Field of Inquiry," *Review of Educational Research* 66 (Fall 1996): 341–359.

32. Goodlad, "Democracy, Education, and Community," p. 120.

33. Pugach and Seidl, "From Exclusion to Inclusion in Urban Schools," p. 392.

34. Sockett, *Moral Base for Teacher Professionalism*, p. 18.

35. See Richard W. Clark, *Effective Professional Development Schools* (San Francisco: Jossey-Bass, 1999).

36. Holmes Group, *Tomorrow's Schools*, p. 1.

37. Holmes Group, *Tomorrow's Schools*, p. 22.

38. Richard W. Clark, "Evaluating Partner Schools: Conceptual Frames, Practical Applications," Occasional Paper no. 18 (Seattle: Center for Educational Renewal, University of Washington, 1994), pp. 8–9.

39. National Council for Accreditation of Teacher Education (NCATE), "Draft Standards for Identifying and Supporting Quality Professional Development Schools" (Washington, D.C.: National Council for Accreditation of Teacher Education, September 1997), p. 2.

40. NCATE, "Draft Standards," p. 2.

41. NCATE, "Draft Standards," p. 2.

42. NCATE, "Draft Standards," p. 3.

43. Robert S. Patterson, "Spotlight on Settings: Brigham Young University–Public School Partnership," *Center Correspondent* no. 10 (Seattle: Center for Educational Renewal, University of Washington, April 1996): 2–5, 10–12.

44. Charles W. Case, Kay A. Norlander, and Patricia Weibust, "The Hartford Professional Development Center: Executive Summary" (Storrs: University of Connecticut, June 1997), p. 1.

45. Goodlad, "Toward a Healthy Ecosystem," p. 218.

46. See, among others, Patricia Clifford and Sharon L. Friesen, "A Curious Plan: Managing on the Twelfth," *Harvard Educational Review* 63 (Fall 1993): 339–358; Marilyn Cochran-Smith and Susan L. Lytle (eds.), *Inside/Outside: Teacher Research and Knowledge* (New York: Teachers College Press, 1993); Goodlad, *Educational Renewal*; Dixie Goswami and Peter R. Stillman (eds.), *Reclaiming the Classroom: Teacher Research as an Agency for Change* (Upper Montclair, N.J.: Boynton/Cook, 1987); Susan L. Lytle and Marilyn Cochran-Smith, "Teacher Research as a Way of Knowing," *Harvard Educational Review* 62 (Winter 1992): 447–474; and Sirotnik, "Meaning and Conduct of Inquiry in School-University Partnerships."

47. Sockett, *Moral Base for Teacher Professionalism*, p. 28.

48. See, as an example, *Educational Researcher* 26 (October 1997), especially Robert Glaser, Ann Lieberman, and Richard Anderson, "'The Vision Thing': Educational Research and AERA in the 21st Century, Part 3: Perspectives on the Research-Practice Relationship," pp. 24–25; Mary M. Kennedy, "The Connection between Research and Practice," pp. 4–12; and Jon Wagner, "The Unavoidable Intervention of Educational Research: A Framework for Reconsidering Researcher-Practitioner Cooperation," pp. 13–22.

49. Goodlad, *Educational Renewal*, p. 271.

50. Abrams, "Internship Summary."

51. Daniel Chase, "Internship Summary" (student paper, School of Education, University of Connecticut, Storrs, May 1997).

52. Chase, "Internship Summary."

53. Kathaleen Moran, "Final Internship Analysis" (student paper, School of Education, University of Connecticut, Storrs, May 1997).

54. Teacher interview, 1994.

55. Martin Semmel, journal entry (student paper, School of Education, University of Connecticut, Storrs, April 25, 1996).

56. Teacher interview, 1994.

57. Sockett, *Moral Base for Teacher Professionalism*.

58. Athena Neilson, "Internship Summary" (student paper, School of Education, University of Connecticut, Storrs, December 1996).

Chapter Five

1. John Dewey, *Democracy and Education* (New York: Macmillan, 1916), p. 357.

2. Council of Economic Advisors for the President's Initiative on Race, *Changing America: Indicators of Social and Economic Well-Being by Race and Hispanic Origin* (Washington, D.C.: Council of Economic Advisors for the President's Initiative on Race, September 1998), p. 4.

3. Maurice Craft, "Cultural Diversity and Teacher Education," in Maurice Craft (ed.), *Teacher Education in Plural Societies: An International Review* (London: Falmer, 1996), p. 1.

4. Henry Louis Gates, Jr., *Loose Canons: Notes on the Culture Wars* (New York: Oxford University Press, 1992), p. xv.

5. Kathaleen Moran, "Final Internship Summary" (student paper, School of Education, University of Connecticut, Storrs, May 1997).

6. bell hooks, *Teaching to Transgress: Education as the Practice of Freedom* (New York: Routledge, 1994), p. 36.

7. Lorianne Brown, "Internship Description" (student paper, School of Education, University of Connecticut, Storrs, December 1995).

8. Marilyn Cochran-Smith, "Uncertain Allies: Understanding the Boundaries of Race and Teaching," *Harvard Educational Review* 65 (Winter 1995): 542.

9. Sandra Finney and Jeff Orr, "'I've Really Learned a Lot, But . . .':
Cross-Cultural Understanding and Teacher Education in a Racist
Society," *Journal of Teacher Education* 46 (November–December
1995): 332.

10. Jill Jacobsen, e-mail response to Professor Pamela Campbell's seminar, February 1996.

11. Daniel J. Broderick III, "Internship Summary" (student paper,
School of Education, University of Connecticut, Storrs, May 1994).

12. Brian Keating, "Internship Summary" (student paper, School of Education, University of Connecticut, Storrs, December 1993).

13. Daniel J. Broderick III, "The Portrayal of a Teacher in an Urban
High School" (student paper, School of Education, University of
Connecticut, Storrs, May 1994), p. 1.

14. Julie Lafontaine, "Dropout Prevention: Is It Worth It? An Analysis
of a Dropout Prevention Program at an Urban High School, A Case
Study" (student paper, School of Education, University of Connecticut, Storrs, May 1995), p. 1.

15. Jennifer A. Del Conte, "An Urban High School Tutorial Program:
The Effect on Student Academic Achievement, Attendance, Attitude and Self-Esteem" (student paper, School of Education, University of Connecticut, Storrs, May 1996), p. 1.

16. Teacher interview, June 1994.

17. Charles W. Case, "The View from Here: Correspondents from
NNER Sites Reflect on the Situation as They See It," *Center Correspondent* no. 5 (Seattle: Center for Educational Renewal, University
of Washington, October 1993): 21.

18. Jill McLean Taylor, Carol Gilligan, and Amy Sullivan, *Between
Voice and Silence: Women and Girls, Race and Relationship* (Cambridge, Mass.: Harvard University Press, 1995), p. 11.

19. Mary Anna Lundeberg, "You Guys Are Overreacting: Teaching
Prospective Teachers About Subtle Gender Bias," *Journal of Teacher
Education* 48 (January–February 1997): 55–61.

20. Patricia B. Campbell and Jo Sanders, "Uninformed But Interested:
Findings of a National Survey on Gender Equity in Preservice

Teacher Education," *Journal of Teacher Education* 48 (January–February 1997): 69.

21. Kerri Kearney, journal entry (student paper, School of Education, University of Connecticut, Storrs, December 1995).

22. Jill Horila, journal entry for Pamela Campbell's seminar (student paper, School of Education, University of Connecticut, Storrs, March 1996).

23. Timothy G. Reagan, "When Is a Language Not a Language? Challenges to 'Linguistic Legitimacy' in Educational Discourse," *Educational Foundations* 11 (Summer 1997): 5–28; and Ira Shor and Paulo Freire, *A Pedagogy for Liberation: Dialogues on Transforming Education* (New York: Bergin & Garvey, 1987).

24. See James Cummins, *Negotiating Identities: Education for Empowerment in a Diverse Society* (Ontario, Calif.: California Association for Bilingual Education, 1996), for a discussion of language and empowerment.

25. Timothy Reagan, "The Case for Applied Linguistics in Teacher Education," *Journal of Teacher Education* 48 (May–June 1997): 192.

26. See Timothy G. Reagan, "Educational Linguistics in Teacher Education" (paper presented at the annual meeting of the American Association of Colleges for Teacher Education, Chicago, February 22, 1996).

27. Richard Abrams, interview, May 1994.

28. Richard Abrams, "Internship Summary" (student paper, School of Education, University of Connecticut, Storrs, May 1994).

29. Abrams, interview, May 1994.

30. John I. Goodlad, "Access to Knowledge," in John I. Goodlad and Thomas C. Lovitt (eds.), *Integrating General and Special Education* (New York: Macmillan, 1993), p. 3.

31. Goodlad and Lovitt (eds.), *Integrating General and Special Education*, p. v.

32. See, among others, David G. Imig, foreword to Linda P. Blanton and others (eds.), *Teacher Education in Transition: Collaborative Programs to Prepare General and Special Educators* (Denver: Love, 1997);

Marleen C. Pugach, "The National Education Reports and Special Education: Implications for Teacher Preparation," *Exceptional Children* 53 (January 1987): 308–314; Wayne Sailor, "Special Education in the Restructured School," *Remedial and Special Education* (November–December 1991): 8–22; Mara Sapon-Shevin, "Working Towards Merger Together: Seeing Beyond Distrust and Fear," *Teacher Education and Special Education* 11 (Summer 1988): 103–110; Seymour B. Sarason and John Doris, *Educational Handicap, Public Policy and Social History: A Broadened Perspective on Mental Retardation* (New York: Free Press, 1979); Stan F. Shaw and others, "Special Education and School Reform," in Lyndal M. Bullock and Richard L. Simpson (eds.), *Critical Issues in Special Education: Implications for Personnel Preparation* (Denton: North Texas State University, 1990); Richard L. Simpson, Richard J. Whelan, and Robert H. Zabel, "Special Education Personnel Preparation in the 21st Century: Issues and Strategies," *Remedial and Special Education* 14 (March–April 1993): 7–22; and Judith A. Winn and Linda P. Blanton, "The Call for Collaboration in Teacher Education," in Blanton and others (eds.), *Teacher Education in Transition.*

33. John I. Goodlad and Sharon Field, "Teachers for Renewing Schools," in Goodlad and Lovitt (eds.), *Integrating General and Special Education,* p. 243.

34. Enzo Zocco, "Statement of Philosophy in Exceptionality II" (student paper, School of Education, University of Connecticut, Storrs, December 1995). Used by permission of Pamela Campbell.

35. Student interview, May 1994.

36. Future special educator, "Statement of Philosophy in Exceptionality I" (student paper, School of Education, University of Connecticut, Storrs, December 1995).

37. Future social studies/history teacher, "Statement of Philosophy in Exceptionality I" (student paper, School of Education, University of Connecticut, Storrs, December 1995).

38. Future elementary educator, "Statement of Philosophy in Exceptionality I" (student paper, School of Education, University of Connecticut, Storrs, December 1996).

39. Daniel Chase, "Final Internship Summary" (student paper, School of Education, University of Connecticut, Storrs, May 1997).

40. Sean O'Leary, "Internship Summary" (student paper, School of Education, University of Connecticut, Storrs, May 1997).

41. Kay A. Norlander, faculty field notes (Storrs: School of Education, University of Connecticut, 1991). "My Life Story," quoted in Judy Sweeney (ed.), *Wings* (Storrs: Special Education Technology Lab, A. J. Pappanikou Center on Special Education and Rehabilitation, University of Connecticut, 1991), p. 23.

42. "Graduates Take Their Skills to Help Inner-City Schools," *Hartford Courant*, February 4, 1996.

43. Pamela Pion-Flaherty, speech during presentation of Faculty Teaching Award, University of Connecticut, Storrs, April 1994.

44. Donna Miziasak, interview, May 1994.

45. Future secondary teacher, Exceptionality I final exam excerpt (student paper, School of Education, University of Connecticut, Storrs, October 1996).

46. Susan Crowley, journal entry for Pamela Campbell's seminar (student paper, School of Education, University of Connecticut, Storrs, November 1995).

47. Mary Catherine Bateson, *Composing a Life* (New York: Atlantic Monthly Press, 1989), p. 13.

Chapter Six

1. Henry David Thoreau, "Civil Disobedience," in *Walden and Civil Disobedience*, ed. Owen Thomas (New York: Norton, 1966), p. 225.

2. Robert B. Westbrook, "Public Schooling and American Democracy," in Roger Soder (ed.), *Democracy, Education, and the Schools* (San Francisco: Jossey-Bass, 1996), p. 125.

3. Walter C. Parker, "Curriculum for Democracy," in Soder (ed.), *Democracy, Education, and the Schools*, p. 189.

4. Kristi Maynard, "Final Reflection" (student paper, School of Education, University of Connecticut, Storrs, May 1997).

5. Kenneth A. Sirotnik, "Evaluation in the Ecology of Schooling: The Process of School Renewal," in John I. Goodlad (ed.), *The Ecology of School Renewal: Eighty-Sixth Yearbook of the National Society for the Study of Education* (Chicago: National Society for the Study of Education, 1987), p. 51.

6. Tom Bird, "The Schoolteacher's Portfolio: An Essay on Possibilities," in Jason Millman and Linda Darling-Hammond (eds.), *The New Handbook of Teacher Evaluation: Assessing Elementary and Secondary School Teachers* (Newbury Park, Calif.: Sage, 1990), pp. 241–256.

7. Samuel B. Bacharach, Sharon C. Conley, and Joseph B. Shedd, "A Career Developmental Framework for Evaluating Teachers as Decision-Makers," *Journal of Personnel Evaluation in Education* 1 (September 1987): 181–194; Richard J. Altenbaugh, "Teachers, Their World, and Their Work: A Review of the Idea of 'Professional Excellence' in School Reform Reports," in Christine M. Shea, Ernest Kahane, and Peter Sola (eds.), *The New Servants of Power: A Critique of the 1980s School Reform Movement* (New York: Greenwood Press, 1989), pp. 167–175; and Sharon C. Conley, "Reforming Paper Pushers and Avoiding Free Agents: The Teacher as a Constrained Decision Maker," *Educational Administration Quarterly* 24 (November 1988): 393–404.

8. Milbrey Wallin McLaughlin and R. Scott Pfeifer, *Teacher Evaluation: Improvement, Accountability, and Effective Learning* (New York: Teachers College Press, 1988), p. 3.

9. Donald A. Schön, *The Reflective Practitioner: How Professionals Think in Action* (New York: Basic, 1983); and Donald A. Schön, *Educating the Reflective Practitioner: Toward a New Design for Teaching and Learning in the Professions* (San Francisco: Jossey-Bass, 1987).

10. Conley, "Reforming Paper Pushers."

11. Conley, "Reforming Paper Pushers," p. 397.

12. Patricia Clifford and Sharon L. Friesen, "A Curious Plan: Managing on the Twelfth," *Harvard Educational Review* 63 (Fall 1993): 347.

13. Marleen C. Pugach and Cynthia L. Warger, "Curriculum Considerations," in John I. Goodlad and Thomas C. Lovitt (eds.), *Integrating General and Special Education* (New York: Macmillan, 1993), p. 139.

14. Nel Noddings, *The Challenge to Care in Schools: An Alternative Approach to Education* (New York: Teachers College Press, 1992), pp. 1–2.

15. Maynard, "Final Reflection."

16. Parker, "Curriculum for Democracy," p. 200.

17. David G. Imig, "'Back to School' Concerns," *AACTE Briefs* 19 (August 31, 1998): 2.

18. Clifford and Friesen, "A Curious Plan," p. 347.

Index

A

Abrams, R., 105, 133–134, 145

Academics and teachers, relationship of: and academic competitiveness, 70, 76; and academic disciplines, 68, 70, 76; academic faculty attitudes toward, 67–69, 103, 104, 108–110; and action research status, 44, 104; and the arts and sciences (liberal education), 71, 72, 75–77; and bridging cultural differences, 43–44, 97, 103, 164–165; classroom teacher attitudes toward, 39–40, 97; and education research, academic, 103, 104, 108–110; and inclusive or special education, 122, 135–142, 144, 158–160; and partner schools, 68, 97; and separation of teaching specialties, 122, 136, 137; and subject-specific course work, 78–79; and teacher research, 12–13, 40–42, 103, 110; and "teacher-proofing" of schooling, 12. *See also* Faculty, teacher education program; Partnerships, school-university

Access to knowledge: for diverse populations, 59, 119–120, 127–128; equal and appropriate, 59; and equity and diversity issues, 120–126; lessons in providing, 158–160; the

moral dimension of, 21, 54–55; teacher commitment to, 57–59, 92

Accountability, moral or standards-driven professional, 19–20, 153–154

Action research. *See* Research, action

Advocacy and stewardship, 64–66, 92–93, 162–164

Age of teachers, 34–35, 58

Allen, W., 39

Analysis, logical, 26

Apprenticeship model of teaching, 38, 53

Arthurdale, West Virginia, 88

Arts and sciences: and teacher education, 71, 72, 75–77

Assessment: prescribed, 12; and reflective practice, 45–46, 153

Attitude, learning to change one's, 108, 163

Autonomy of teachers: limited, 11–12, 46; and organizational change, 148–151; in research and teaching, 109; and time use, 31, 64, 108–110. *See also* Decision making, teacher

B

Banquet, a multicultural, 114–116

Bateson, M. C., 146

Belenky, M. F., 75